THE PUTNEY D 1647

Dorian Gerhold

We have been by providence put upon strange things, such as the ancientest here doth scarce remember.
> – *(Edward Sexby, soldier, Putney, 28 October 1647)*

... really I think that the poorest he that is in England hath a life to live as the greatest he; and therefore truly, Sir, I think it's clear, that every man that is to live under a Government ought first by his own consent to put himself under that Government.
> – *(Thomas Rainborough, colonel, Putney, 29 October 1647)*

Note on the extracts: The extracts are taken from C.H. Firth, The Clarke Papers *(1992 edn.). Spelling and capitalisation are modernised and punctuation is occasionally added. Omissions are not indicated. Parts of the transcript make little sense without editorial changes; here the occasional word or two added (almost invariably following Firth) is not indicated, but longer additions or less certain ones are in square brackets. Words in square brackets in italics are explanatory notes. The extracts account for about a fifth of the original transcript. For the sake of consistency, the spelling of extracts from the transcript elsewhere in the present book is also modernised, though the spelling in quotations from other documents is not. In Appendix 1, the* Agreement *is printed in full, but with spelling, capitalisation and punctuation modernised.*

Acknowledgements: I am grateful to the following for permission to reproduce illustrations: Clare Melinsky (illustrator) and Rampant Lions (publisher), cover picture; the Provost and Fellows of Worcester College, Oxford, 1, 11; House of Lords Library, 2, 24; the Trustees of the British Museum, 3; National Portrait Gallery, London, 4, 17, 22, 26, 27, 28; British Library, 5, 6, 13; Jim Slade, 8, 9; St Mary's Parochial Church Council, Putney, 10; Cromwell Museum, Huntingdon, 12; Victoria and Albert Museum, London, 14; Michael Bull, 15, 16; Ashmolean Museum, Oxford, 18, 21; Wandsworth Museum, 23; National Maritime Museum, London (BHC2646), 25; Charles Pettiward, 30. Figs. 7, 19, 20 and 31 are from the Olney Collection, prints from which are held by Wandsworth Local History Service and Wandsworth Museum.

I am especially grateful to Professor John Morrill for helpful comments on an earlier draft of the text. Michael Bull also provided helpful advice on the text and illustrations. Any errors which remain are mine alone.

ISBN 978-0-905121-20-8

Published by Dorian Gerhold, 19 Montserrat Road, Putney, SW15 2LD
Printed by Cantate, Culvert Place, Battersea, SW11 5DZ

Contents

Fig. 1 (next page). The first page of William Clarke's transcript of the Putney Debates.

Lieuten: Generall Cromwell.

The Officers being mett, first Sayd,

That this Meeting was for publique businesses, Those that had any thinge to say concerning the publique businesse they might have Libertie to Speake.

Mr Edward Sexby.

one, Allen, one, Lockyer, and my Selfe are 3.

They have sent two Souldiers, out of yor owne Regimt: and one of Col: Whalley's with two other Gentlemen, one Wildman, one Petty.

Comissary Gen: Ireton

That hee had not the paper of what was done uppon all of them.

It was Referrd to the Comittee, That they should consider of the paper that was printed, The Case of the Army Stated, and to Examine the particulars in itt, and to Represent and offer somethinges to this Comittee about itt: they were likewise appointed to send for those psons concernd in this paper. The Comittee mett according to appointment that night. It was only then Resolved on, That there should bee some Sent in a friendlie way (nott by Comand, or Summons) to invite some of those Gentlemen to come in with vs, I thinke,

Mr Sexby.

I was desired by the Lieutent: Generall to know the bottome of their Desires, they gave vs this Answer, That they would willinglie draw them uppe, and represent them vnto you, They are come att this time to tender them to yor Considerations with their Resolutions to maintaine them.

Wee have bin by providence put vppon strange thinges, such as the antecedent heere doth Scarce Remember, The setting to those Ends, providence hath bin with vs, and yet wee have found little of our indeavours, ―

The

Introduction

The Putney Debates are such a familiar part of history that it is easy to forget what an extraordinary event they were. For many days, officers and ordinary soldiers of the New Model Army, ranging in background from gentlemen to button-sellers and shoemakers, debated together how the country should be run, with little sign of deference and as if everyone's opinion mattered. No army has ever behaved like this before or since. Many of the participants spoke as if they were starting with a clean sheet from first principles, and ideas then revolutionary, such as giving the vote to all men and abolishing the monarchy's powers, were put forward and were taken seriously, even by those who opposed them. And this in a country which less than a decade before had been a hierarchically-organised kingdom with a powerful monarch and aristocracy.

Almost as remarkable is that we have a transcript providing something close to the actual words spoken – despite its imperfections a better record than we have for the parliaments of this period. The transcript captures the spontaneous and often passionate nature of the debate. As one historian wrote when the documents were rediscovered in the 1890s, 'they ... bring us, as we have never been brought before, into the very heart of that army in the midst of which Cromwell lived and moved'.

The Debates raise many questions. Why were the Army's officers so willing to listen to ordinary soldiers? Why was it the Army which was debating how the country should be governed? What were the Debates intended to achieve? Why did the Army debate radical proposals put forward by a largely civilian group, the Levellers, and allow some of those civilians to participate in an Army meeting? Why did Cromwell allow the Levellers to take up so much of the time available? Was there ever a realistic prospect of ideas such as votes for all being adopted? And what, if anything, was the outcome of the Debates? The aim of this book is to set the Putney Debates in context, to answer those questions (as far as possible), and to convey the flavour and range of the Debates by means of extracts from the transcript.

Fig. 2. The New Model Army arrayed for battle: Naseby, 1645 (detail).

Background to the Debates

The New Model Army

The army which conducted the Debates was a latecomer in the Civil War between King Charles I and Parliament, though it incorporated many existing regiments. The war had begun in 1642 over issues such as the arbitrary powers of the Crown and the King's innovations in the Church. The New Model Army had its origins in the situation in late 1644. Parliament's forces, allied with the Scots, had inflicted a crushing defeat on the King at Marston Moor in July 1644, but Parliament's victory was not followed up. The Earl of Manchester, general of one of the main parliamentary armies, appeared reluctant to challenge the Royalists, probably because he wanted a negotiated peace and feared the consequences of a total parliamentary victory. Parliamentarians began to polarise into a peace party, including the Earls of Manchester and Essex, and a party which was determined to win the war, including Oliver Cromwell.

In December 1644 the Commons agreed a Self-Denying Ordinance, requiring members of both Houses to lay down their commands or (in the case of Commons members) to resign their seats. From the war party's point of view this would exclude the two main peace-party commanders (Essex and Manchester) at the cost of Cromwell's own command. However the Lords stood by Essex and blocked it. The war party then, in January 1645, put forward the New Model Ordinance, which would combine Parliament's three largest armies into a new southern army with a new commander and new officers. Sir Thomas Fairfax was appointed as commander-in-chief. The Lords eventually gave way both on the New Model Army and the Self-Denying Ordinance, but Cromwell's commission was temporarily extended and he was eventually made permanent as lieutenant-general of cavalry.

The new army was like other Civil War armies in that it suffered heavily from desertions. The infantry, in particular, were drawn from the lowest ranks of society, and tended to desert as quickly as they could. The cavalry were different: they tended to be the sons of yeomen and craftsmen, serving voluntarily. It was the 5,000 or 6,000 cavalry and about 7,000 of the foot who served for longer periods who gave the Army its peculiar character. There is no doubt that the core of the Army, albeit the officers more consistently than the rank and file, was strongly imbued with religious enthusiasm. Much time was spent praying, fasting, discussing the Bible, sharing their religious experiences and listening to or even delivering sermons. Few army commanders in history would willingly have listened to a former apprentice grocer, Lieutenant-Colonel Goffe, reflecting on the relevance of the Book of Revelation to their situation, as these did at Putney, and not many armies have seriously considered disbanding in order to prevent further bloodshed, as this one did in 1648.

Religious enthusiasm had several practical consequences: high morale, a sense of fellowship and unity, a degree of egalitarianism (reflected in the participation of the rank and file at Putney), a sense of separateness from the rest of society, a strict code of personal conduct (exemplified by the harsh punishment for blasphemy – boring of the tongue with a red hot iron), courage and ruthlessness.

The New Model Army quickly proved effective. It won a major victory at Naseby in June 1645, followed by further victories, which gave it a reputation of invincibility. Oxford, the King's headquarters, surrendered in June 1646, and the first Civil War was virtually over, at least in England.

The revolt of the Army

What everyone expected next was a peace agreement with the King and the disbanding of the parliamentary armies or the bulk of them. This did not happen, for two reasons. First, the King had no intention of negotiating seriously, and merely played for time while seeking to divide his enemies and raise further forces. Secondly, the way that the dominant Presbyterian grouping in Parliament sought to disband the New Model Army provoked it into defiance.

In 1646 Parliament was becoming polarised into two parties somewhat different from the peace and war parties: the Presbyterians, who intended to fulfil earlier promises to Parliament's Scottish allies to impose a Presbyterian ecclesiastical system on England and wanted a conservative political settlement and the crushing of religious dissent, and the Independents, who believed in greater freedom of conscience for Protestants and wanted to retain strong forces until a peace settlement was agreed. Once the military threat from the King was removed, and even more after the Scottish army began marching home on 30 January 1647, removing another potential threat, the Presbyterians became dominant in Parliament.

Parliament needed to respond to the overwhelming desire in the country to reduce the burdens of war, including heavy taxation, the free quarter of troops, political centralisation and disorder. These were giving rise to dangerous unrest, which was eventually to erupt into a second Civil War in 1648. The key to reducing the burdens was disbandment of the armies, but this was complicated by the Presbyterians' attitude towards the New Model Army, whose religious radicalism it detested.

The New Model Army accounted for less than half of Parliament's troops. Military considerations favoured disbanding the less effective provincial forces first and retaining strong forces until a peace settlement was agreed. Parliament proposed instead to begin by sending part of the New Model Army, under new commanders, to fight rebels in Ireland and disbanding the rest, without first addressing their grievances.

These grievances were, above all, arrears of pay and the need for an indemnity for acts committed during the war. Without an indemnity disbanded soldiers would

Events in 1647

Jan	30	Scottish army begins marching home
Feb	19	Commons votes to reduce military establishment in England to 6,400
Mar	6	Commons votes to send 12,600 from New Model to Ireland
	18	First evidence of a soldiers' petition
	29	Commons passes 'Declaration of Dislike'
Apr	15	First evidence of agitators
	27	*Vindication of the Officers of the Army* presented to the Commons
May	15/16	Meetings at Saffron Walden to agree a statement of the Army's grievances
	18	Commons decides on immediate disbandment of New Model
	20	Cromwell assures the Commons that the New Model will disband if so ordered
	25	Commons votes for disbandment to be on 1-15 June
	29	Petition to Fairfax calling for a general rendezvous; Fairfax agrees
June	2	Cornet Joyce seizes the King
	4	Cromwell throws in his lot with the Army
	4/5	General rendezvous at Kentford Heath; *Solemn Engagement of the Army* agreed by all regiments
	14	Army's *Declaration*, making political demands
July	8	Soldiers of Parliament's northern army join the revolt
	16/17	First meetings of General Council, at Reading; *Heads of the Proposals* discussed
	17	All land forces in England and Wales placed by Parliament under Fairfax's command
	20	Eleven leading Presbyterians permitted by the Commons to withdraw
	26	Mob takes control of Commons and Lords
Aug	4-7	Army occupies London
	24	King moved to Hampton Court
	26	Army headquarters moves to Putney
Sept	9	First meeting of General Council in Putney church
	29	New agents first recorded
Oct	18	New agents present *The Case of the Armie* to Fairfax
	21	General Council considers *The Case*
	27	Everard brings the *Agreement of the People* to Army headquarters
	28	Putney Debates day 1
	29	Putney Debates day 2
Nov	1	Putney Debates day 3
	2	General Council endorses committee's decisions on the franchise etc.
	8	General Council agrees to send agitators back to regiments
	9	Last meeting of General Council with soldier agitators
	11	King escapes from Hampton Court
	11	New agents and Sexby call on soldiers to disobey summons to separate rendezvous
	15	First rendezvous, at Ware; mutiny suppressed
	17	Army headquarters leaves Putney

Fig. 3. The House of Commons, sitting in St Stephen's Chapel, Westminster, as shown on the Great Seal of the Commonwealth of 1651.

be harried in the courts over acts such as the seizure of horses, which was a hanging offence. But what seems to have been most resented was the clear hostility of the Presbyterians towards the army which had won the war for Parliament. Even so, the Presbyterians' plan might well have succeeded had they dealt with the Army's material grievances earlier, avoided insulting it and sent it to Ireland with its existing commanders.

The Army's officers, who at this stage included many Presbyterians, were divided, and neither Fairfax nor Cromwell questioned Parliament's authority until the end of May, but there was great solidarity among the soldiers, keenly aware of the need for unity in the face of the threat against them, and this was what saved the Army. A petition began to be circulated. When it came to Parliament's attention,

Fig. 4. Sir Thomas Fairfax, commander-in-chief of the New Model Army from 1645 to 1650.

the Presbyterians fuelled the flames by passing on 29 March what became known as the 'Declaration of Dislike', declaring anyone who continued petitioning to be 'enemies of the state and disturbers of the public peace'. Vindication of the Army's honour became a new demand from the soldiers. Whereas in March they were seeking only to remedy their grievances as soldiers, their demands would gradually become more political to meet the threat from their enemies in Parliament.

Meanwhile even the men in regiments whose officers had agreed to serve in Ireland were refusing to go. In April regiments began to elect agents or 'agitators' – two or more for each regiment. This began in the cavalry, the more literate and politically-conscious part of the Army, taking root first at the level of the troop (about a hundred men) and involving the troop officers (captains, lieutenants and cornets); the foot companies followed in May. Inter-regimental organisation soon developed, capable of taking action without the senior officers. Organisation by soldiers, usually connected with arrears of pay, was not uncommon in the sixteenth and seventeenth centuries; what was new was the sophistication of the organisation and the range of objectives.

The Commons decided on 18 May that disbandment should proceed as soon as possible, and a week later that it should take place at separate rendezvous on 1-15 June. The soldiers' material grievances were to be dealt with, but the 'Declaration of Dislike' was not withdrawn. The Presbyterians still had access to various forces, including the northern army, the London trained bands and a large number of ex-soldiers (the 'Reformadoes'), and were negotiating with the Scots in case of trouble. It was still not clear that the New Model Army would resist.

However, with disbandment imminent, parts of the Army were starting to take independent action to avert it. Ireton noted the soldiers' view that 'if they be thus scornfully dealt with for their faithful service whilst the sword is in their hands, what should their usage be when they are dissolved?' At Bury St Edmunds on 29 May a petition supported by the great majority of the Army's officers was presented to Fairfax, calling for a general rendezvous of the whole Army, making clear that it would go ahead even without his consent and demanding redress of grievances before disbandment.

The senior officers now faced a choice between rejecting Parliament's commands or losing control over the Army. Fairfax made the momentous decision to defy Parliament and preserve the Army's unity. On 2 June Cornet Joyce took control of the King (in collusion with the generals but without a direct order); on 4 June Cromwell threw in his lot with the Army; and on 4-5 June the Army held its rendezvous at Kentford Heath, near Newmarket. There it agreed a 'Solemn Engagement', pledging not to disband until it was satisfied on stated matters, and effectively demanding the removal of the leading Presbyterian Members who had abused the Army.

The system of agitators was now formalised by establishing the General Council of the Army, consisting of two officers and two soldiers elected by each regiment, together with the general officers. Decisions in the General Council were to be by

11

The manner of His Excellency Sir *Thomas Fairfax*, and the Officers of His Armie sitting in COVNCELL.

Fig. 5. Fairfax presiding in 1647 in the Army's Council of War, which consisted of 30 or so officers of the rank of major or above and advised him on military matters.

majority vote. The purpose of the General Council was to ensure that the Solemn Engagement was complied with and, by giving the agitators a voice, to make it possible to restore discipline and preserve unity. Thus the General Council in which the Putney Debates were conducted and in which ordinary soldiers participated arose out of the specific circumstances of spring 1647, when the unity of the soldiers and the co-operation of most of their officers had saved the Army from disbandment.

The march on London

The Army had acted for self-protection, and had no intention of supplanting Parliament, but in order to maintain pressure on Parliament it began to advance towards London, where the Presbyterians were believed (correctly) to be planning an armed force of their own. From mid-June to mid-July Parliament alternated between defiance and conciliation, and the Army alternately advanced and withdrew. On 14 June the Army made its famous declaration that it was 'not a mere mercenary army' but had been summoned by Parliament 'to the defence of [its] own and the people's just rights and liberties'. For the first time it made clear political demands, including a purge of both Houses, more frequent elections and a redrawing of parliamentary constituencies to make them more equal (reflecting a belief that the Commons needed to be made more representative). It began to achieve results, including action on the material grievances, expunging of the

Declaration of Dislike and, on 20 July, permission from the Commons for the 11 Presbyterian Members the Army wanted suspended to withdraw overseas.

A complicating factor was the need to reach agreement with the King. Such an agreement, on almost any terms, would have been immensely popular in the country, but if secured by Parliament might betray what the Army believed it had fought for. The Army therefore began working on its own proposals. The draft prepared by senior officers, known as the Heads of the Proposals, was less harsh towards the King than Parliament's terms (as well as omitting the establishment of a Presbyterian church), and included reforms such as regular two-year parliaments, more equal allocation of parliamentary seats, a right to petition and law reform. The draft was first discussed at a meeting of the General Council at Reading on 17 July. An agreement between Army and King would have been hard for parliamentary opponents to resist.

However, the King continued to play for time and the Army's successes were causing a reaction among the Presbyterians, especially in the City of London. On 26 July a mob, probably organised by some of the Presbyterian leaders, invaded the two Houses and effectively took them captive. The two Speakers and many Members and Peers took refuge with the Army. The Presbyterian leaders, back in Parliament, began to mobilise forces and invited the King to London. Now the Army had no alternative to the occupation of London, which it carried out on 4 August. The threatened armed resistance quickly evaporated.

The Army had demonstrated its power and had removed a military threat and the Presbyterian leaders in Parliament, but it still faced the same underlying problems: a House of Commons in which, despite the removal of their leaders, the Presbyterians could still command majorities, and a King whose good faith in negotiations seemed increasingly doubtful. It was still committed to working with Parliament (though it called on both Houses to expel Members who had betrayed their trust) and to a settlement with the King. When Major White declared at a General Council at Putney in September that there was no visible authority in the kingdom but the power of the sword, this was regarded as so shocking that he was immediately expelled. A major purpose of meetings of the General Council, in addition to enabling grievances to be raised, was to agree peace terms which could be put to the King and Parliament with the support of the whole Army.

On 26 August the Army moved its headquarters from Kingston to Putney – as one newspaper put it, 'more neere to London, by reason of the better expedition of businesse betwixt the Parliament and Army'. It was close enough to London to put pressure on Parliament and prevent hostile forces being raised, but not overtly intimidating. The Army's headquarters remained at Putney for 11 weeks, until 17 November, though most regiments were stationed elsewhere.

Putney in 1647

Putney in 1647 was a small Thames-side town of about 900 people, strung out along the High Street and the nearby parts of the river bank. Its closeness to London, just six miles away and easily accessible by horse, coach or boat, not only attracted the Army in 1647 but also largely determined the character of the place. One aspect of this was that about 40% of the householders employed locally were described as watermen. The watermen worked on the cross-river ferry to Fulham (there was no bridge yet), on the 'long ferry' to London and in goods transport, and the Army must have provided good business for them. Putney's strategic position had been demonstrated in 1642, when the Earl of Essex built a bridge of boats across the Thames there.

The other aspect of London's closeness was that it attracted gentlemen, office-

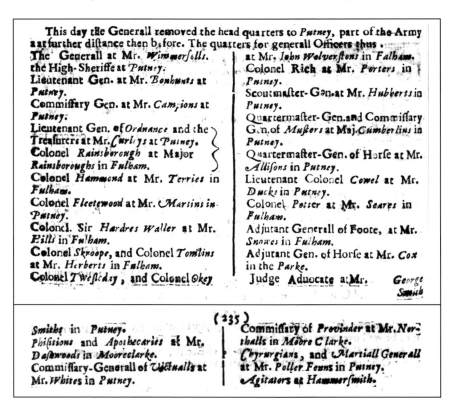

Fig. 6. List of the quarters of the senior Army officers at Putney in 1647, from Perfect Occurrences, *27 August-3 September. See Appendix 3.*

Fig. 7. Henry Campion's house at Putney, in which Commissary General Ireton was billetted in 1647. It stood on the south side of Putney Bridge Road close to the High Street.

holders and merchants, who occupied the 16 or so large houses and tended to use them as summer houses or for long weekends. The inhabitants of these houses dominated the town, owning most of the land, employing most of the people, either as servants or tradesmen, and controlling the parish vestry, which dealt with matters such as poor relief. In 1657 it was said that Putney might have a considerable influence on the City of London 'by reason of the quality of the cittizens of greate worth and value in the said towne'.

Putney had experienced several upheavals as a result of the war. Soldiers had passed through or been billetted, several times bringing plague with them. The most important landholder, Sir Thomas Dawes, whose father Sir Abraham had done extremely well out of the King as a farmer of the customs, suffered heavy fines and long imprisonments, and was to lose most of his lands. Putney's Minister, Richard Avery, had been ejected as a supporter of the catholicising tendency favoured by the King known as Arminianism, and after several short-lived appointments the Minister from 1646 to 1649 was Edward Houghton, a Presbyterian.

What Putney's inhabitants thought of the Army in their midst is not recorded, but they no doubt bitterly resented having soldiers billetted upon them without being paid for it. Only in a few cases are the inhabitants' allegiances known. For example, Thomas Chamberlain, whose house was to play an important role during the Debates, was a Presbyterian, at least by 1659. Some of the richer inhabitants probably avoided the Army by staying in their London houses.

There were plenty of attractive billets for officers both in Putney and Fulham, though many of those listed in a contemporary newspaper cannot be identified. Fairfax stayed at William Wymondsold's, which was almost certainly the house built by Sir Abraham Dawes on what is now the site of Putney Station – the largest house in Putney. Cromwell lodged at 'Mr Bonhunt's'. No Bonhunt appears in any contemporary records, and this was probably Thomas Bownest, but where he lived is unknown. Henry Ireton, who played such a prominent part in the Debates,

15

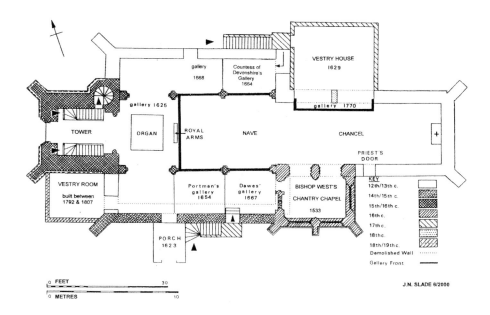

Fig. 8. Plan of St.Mary's church, Putney, before it was rebuilt in 1836, drawn by Jim Slade.

Fig. 9. Plan showing the relationship of the pre-1836 church to the existing one, drawn by Jim Slade.

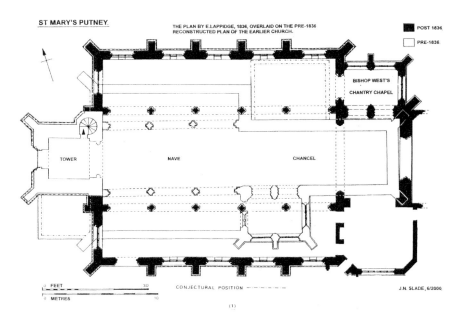

Fig. 10. Nicholas Lane's map of Putney in 1636. North is to the right.

stayed at Henry Campion's near the corner of the High Street and Putney Bridge Road. Thomas Rainborough was able to stay at his brother's house in Fulham. The agitators lodged at Hammersmith, and presumably passed to and fro on the river, but they met at least once at Hugh Hubbert's house near Putney church (in the High Street opposite the present cinema, just south of Weimar Street). While the Army's headquarters were at Putney officers and soldiers must have been a familiar sight on the streets, and a great deal of political debate must have taken place in houses great and small. Cromwell and Ireton examined one of the King's answers to peace proposals 'in a garden-house at Putney'.

Putney's church, St Mary's, stood by the river. Its successor still stands there (by the bridge), and the tower, Bishop West's chapel (re-sited) and the columns and arches (also re-sited) have survived from the church used by the Army in 1647. It had been greatly restored 20 years earlier, when the first of many galleries was added to cope with the rising population. It was crammed with pews, many of them reserved for the occupants of the great houses, and was intended to enable people to see and hear the preaching of sermons delivered from a pulpit, rather than for large numbers of people to hold debates. At an earlier meeting of the General Council in Reading over a hundred people had been present. The clearest space at Putney was undoubtedly the chancel, where there was a communion table surrounded by 'kneeling benches', and one newspaper records the General Council meeting 'about the communion table'. On the other hand the chancel was only 15 feet wide, and if the Debates took place there the participants (especially those not recorded as speaking) must have spilled out into the nave. Important Army meetings often took place in churches, partly because they were usually the largest buildings available, but perhaps also reflecting the belief that they were engaged in God's work. From 9 September the General Council met every Thursday in Putney church.

New agents and Levellers

The new agents

For much of September there was a large degree of consensus in the Army, since all shared a desire for a peace agreement and the Army was achieving its aims in areas such as indemnity. But there was resentment against the Presbyterian majority in Parliament and the lack of progress in reform, and increasing distrust of the King and of what might be agreed in negotiations with him. On 22 September Colonel Rainborough proposed in the Commons that there be no further addresses to the King.

In late September five cavalry regiments, all noted for their religious radicalism and political awareness, elected new agitators or agents. Their status was ambiguous: some seem to have been existing agitators, while others may never have been regularly elected and did not replace the existing agitators. Also, some existing agitators, such as Edward Sexby, seem to have been closely associated with them. On 9 October the new agents put their names to *The Case of the Armie Truly Stated* (of which Sexby may well have been the main author), and this began the train of events leading to the Debates.

The Levellers

The role of the Levellers (if any) in the emergence of the new agents is unclear. The Levellers emerged from the ferment of ideas that developed after censorship broke down during the Civil Wars, and were predominantly London-based civilians. It was only around the time of the Debates that they were becoming an organised movement, and only then that they became known as Levellers – a term of abuse implying that they wanted to level all distinctions of rank or property.

The Levellers have been aptly described as 'the first democratic political movement in modern history', unmatched in any country until the late eighteenth century. Their central political idea was that all power originated in the people, who entrusted their elected representatives with as much of it as they chose, subjecting even the sovereign legislative body to frequent elections and to fundamental laws which could not be altered by statute. Other demands included equality of all before the law, drastic reform of the legal system, abolition of all monopolies, abolition of tithes, protection for religious sects against Presbyterian intolerance and more equitable taxation. At the time of the Putney Debates they were still working out whether anyone (e.g. servants and beggars) should be excluded from the franchise.

In March 1647 the Levellers presented their 'large petition' to the Commons, which responded in May by ordering that the petition be publicly burnt by the common hangman. Having no prospect of influencing Parliament, they were obviously keen to influence the Army once it became an independent political force. The Army's leaders sometimes found them useful, and the two Levellers who spoke at Putney had also been involved at Reading in devising the Heads of the Proposals. There was agreement on some specific issues, such as the right to petition, and some Leveller ideas clearly had powerful appeal in the Army.

But the Levellers' influence in the Army was limited by the fact that the soldiers needed a strong central authority to provide their pay and arrears and secure their indemnity, whereas the Levellers proposed a much weaker central authority, and also, eventually, by the disunity they caused in the Army. Most of the soldiers were consistently interested only in the issues which affected them as soldiers. Also the religious radicals in the Army and elsewhere tended to be more interested in rule by the saints than in rule by all men. Nevertheless, the Levellers do seem to have worked with the new agents on the documents which gave rise to the Putney Debates, almost certainly inspiring the proposal for a wider franchise, two of them participated in the Debates at the invitation of the new agents, and they mounted a serious challenge to the Army's leaders over the Army's political aims and, eventually, over control of the Army.

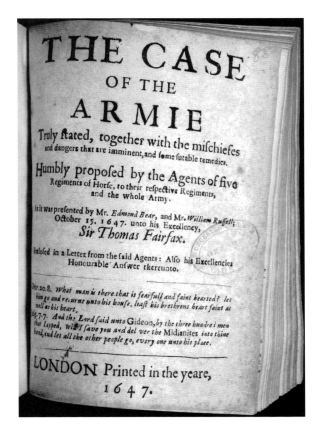

Fig. 11. Title page of William Clarke's copy of The Case of the Armie Truly Stated. *Note the quotations from the Bible.*

Fig. 12. Oliver Cromwell.

The Case *and the* Agreement

The Case of the Armie Truly Stated largely reflected concerns within the Army, but had some sections suggesting Leveller involvement. The central thrust of much of it was that there had been a failure to honour the Army's commitments, not so much because of failings within the Army but because of corrupt and hard-hearted Members of Parliament. It called on the Army to break off negotiations and impose a settlement, and for an immediate purge of Parliament, dissolution of Parliament within ten months, elections every two years, more equal distribution of seats and a much wider franchise, including 'all the free-born' aged 21 or over except 'delinquents' (i.e. Royalists). Some of this reflected what the Army had been calling for since June and could be accommodated within the Army consensus, but not the imposition of a settlement or the wider franchise.

The General Council discussed *The Case* on 21 October and referred it to a committee for consideration. The initial intention of the senior officers seems to have been to punish those who had submitted it for creating division in the Army, but they evidently changed their minds, no doubt assisted by the fact that the committee included Sexby and others of similar views. The pamphlet's authors were asked 'in a friendlie way (nott by command or summons)' to attend the General Council to explain their position. On 27 October Robert Everard, one of the new agents, brought to Army headquarters not just a reply to the General Council's objections but also *An Agreement of the People*, justly one of the most famous Civil War pamphlets.

The *Agreement* was clearly a Leveller pamphlet, possibly drafted by John Wildman, even though put forward in the names of the new agents. It seems to have been written on that very day to exploit the opportunity to present views to the Army. Some of its proposals were similar to those in earlier Army documents, such as two-year parliaments and a redistribution of parliamentary seats (though its call for redistribution 'according to the number of the inhabitants' implied that all adult males would have the vote). But it was much more radical than any previous proposals considered by the Army (including *The Case)* in three ways. First, it introduced the idea of a written constitution to be subscribed to by all adult males. Unlike the demands in *The Case*, this was a bottom-up constitution sweeping away every existing institution and could only be part of an imposed settlement, rather than one agreed with Parliament and the King. Secondly it introduced the concept of powers that were reserved to the people alone and could not be altered by Parliament. These were to include 'matters of religion', equality before the law and the soldiers' indemnity. Thirdly, it called for the House of Commons to be supreme (subject to the reserved powers), leaving little or no role for the King and the Lords.

On reading the *Agreement*, Cromwell perceived 'that there were new designes a driving' and decided that its sponsors should be invited to explain their intentions to the General Council on the following day, 28 October. Apparently the Army's

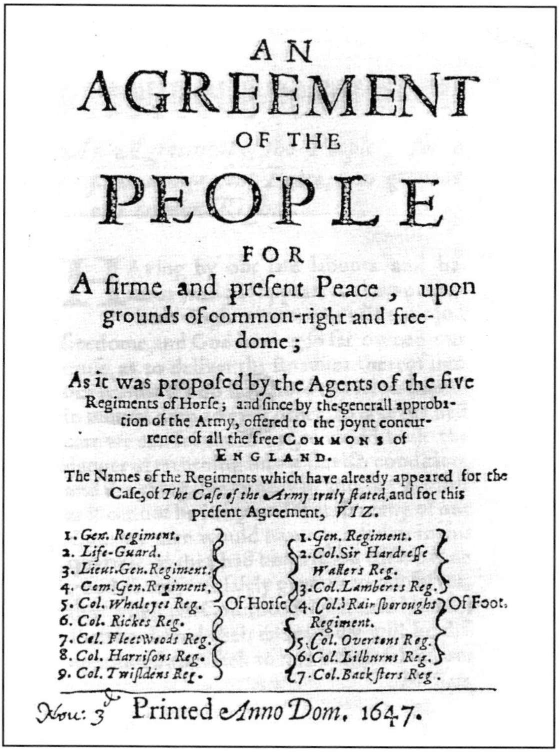

AN
AGREEMENT
OF THE
PEOPLE
FOR
A firme and preſent Peace, upon grounds of common-right and free-dome;
As it was propoſed by the Agents of the five Regiments of Horſe; and ſince by the generall approbation of the Army, offered to the joynt concurrence of all the free COMMONS of ENGLAND.
The Names of the Regiments which have already appeared for the Caſe, of *The Caſe of the Army truly ſtated*, and for this preſent Agreement, *VIZ.*

Of Horſe:
1. *Gen. Regiment.*
2. *Life-Guard.*
3. *Lieut.Gen.Regiment.*
4. *Com.Gen.Regiment,*
5. *Col. Whaleyes Reg.*
6. *Col. Rickes Reg.*
7. *Col. Fleetwoods Reg.*
8. *Col. Harriſons Reg.*
9. *Col. Twiſdens Reg.*

Of Foot:
1. *Gen. Regiment.*
2. *Col.Sir Hardreſſe Wallers Reg.*
3. *Col.Lamberts Reg.*
4. *Col. Rainſboroughs Regiment.*
5. *Col. Overtons Reg.*
6. *Col. Lilburns Reg.*
7. *Col.Backſters Reg.*

Nou: 3 Printed *Anno Dom.* 1647.

Fig. 13. Title page of An Agreement of the People. *The paper was not printed until about 3 November. 'By the generall approbation of the Army' may have been a tendentious reference to the discussion in the General Council.*

leaders had been manoeuvred into direct confrontation with a rival organisation over radical proposals. However, while the *Agreement* was clearly perceived as divisive, it was presented by soldiers and may not have been seen as a Leveller tract, the Levellers who turned up next day to defend it were probably not yet seen as part of an organised movement, and the Levellers as a whole were probably not yet seen as the danger they became later. Those who argued for radical ideas at Putney were certainly not an organised group: Rainborough seems to have been acting independently, and Sexby was never a Leveller (showing at Putney far more interest in *The Case* than the *Agreement*). Cromwell may well have believed that unity could be restored through debate (rather than punishment), and under-estimated the appeal some of the proposals, such as a wider franchise, would have within the Army. Perhaps he also wanted to be certain that God was not speaking through the new agents; as Goffe put it during the Debates, 'let us take heed of rejecting any of the saints of God before God rejects them'.

As for the new agents, presenting the *Agreement* may have been a tactical error, since it generated fierce debate, made it harder to reach agreement on the proposals in *The Case* and caused them to be regarded as divisive.

The Debates

The General Council or its committees met daily at Putney from 28 October to 11 November, but only three days at the beginning are fully (or almost fully) recorded, and only two of these were formal meetings of the General Council. Probably a record was seen as potentially useful for preventing subsequent misrepresentation.

Fairfax was having one of his frequent illnesses during the recorded Debates, so Cromwell presided. As indicated above, there may have been over a hundred people present, and it needs to be remembered that the issues were debated before a large audience, who had to be persuaded, rather than by a handful of participants cosily seated around a communion table. There is no list of those who attended; all we have is the names of those who spoke. These show that only a minority of the participants actually spoke, and indicate that those who did were not necessarily typical of the Army's views. There were 34 speakers, and another 46 participants were named as members of committees, but the dominant figures were Cromwell and Ireton for the senior officers and Rainborough and Wildman supporting the more radical ideas. Although it is clear that those present felt they could speak freely, only five ordinary soldiers spoke, all from cavalry regiments – Sexby, Lockyer and William Allen among the agitators, and Everard (at first recorded as 'Buffcoat') and a 'Bedfordshire man' among the new agents. The latter two, attending by invitation rather than right, may have been the only new agents present. On the other hand soldier agitators were well represented on committees. Only 12 of about 50 officer agitators spoke, many only once and briefly. The divisions were certainly not between officers and ordinary soldiers, since many senior officers, such as Rainborough, had radical views.

The presence of two civilians, John Wildman and Maximilian Petty, requires explanation. Wildman in particular is an extraordinary person to find discussing the country's form of government with those who might be determining it – one of English history's greatest and longest-lived plotters. The new agents seem to have brought Wildman and Petty to argue for ideas which had been borrowed from them and which the new agents had put their names to but were perhaps not confident they could defend. As Wildman put it, they 'desired me that I would be their mouth, and in their names to represent their sense unto you'. In this way the General Council, a purely Army body, ended up discussing a Leveller pamphlet with leading Levellers. The other civilian who spoke, Hugh Peter, was an Army chaplain.

Rainborough's presence also requires explanation, and seems to have been accidental. He had been appointed vice-admiral of the fleet a month earlier, and had just heard that his command of a foot regiment had been taken away as a result, so he had come to Putney to protest, apparently having expected to be both vice-admiral and colonel. Strictly, therefore, he was no longer a member of the General Council. He seems to have had no previous association with the Levellers or the

Fig. 14. John Wildman (c.1622-1693), Leveller and plotter, in 1647. (Miniature by John Hoskins the younger).

Fig. 15. St Mary's church, Putney, seen from the south-east in 1797. Apart from changes made necessary by new galleries (one or two of the dormer windows and an external stair), this view would have been the same in 1647. Although the church has been rebuilt, the tower survives, and so, on new sites, do Bishop West's chantry chapel (centre) and the columns and arches inside.

Fig. 16. The interior of St Mary's church, Putney, looking from the chancel towards the west end, before the rebuilding of 1836. The gallery across the west end was built in 1625.

new agents and his active support of Leveller proposals was brief (perhaps stimulated by anger against Cromwell), but he nevertheless uttered the most memorable words at Putney in favour of them.

The clear aim of the Debates, constantly stressed by speakers, was to find a consensus and re-establish unity. This explains some features otherwise puzzling today. The emphasis on keeping to the Army's previous engagements, which dominated the first day, reflected not only the fact that keeping engagements was a matter of honour, but also that these engagements had been agreed by the whole Army, sometimes through the General Council, and were therefore a crucial part of that unity which had saved the Army. They included commitment to restoring the King to at least some of his authority, keeping a role for the House of Lords, pursuing a settlement to be endorsed by Parliament and respecting the planned Presbyterian system (though not making it exclusive). Similarly, attempts to refer matters to a committee were not a delaying tactic but were intended to enable a smaller group to prepare the ground for debate in the somewhat unwieldy General Council. The committees appointed were genuinely representative, including many radicals and ordinary soldiers. The emphasis on seeking the will of God, through prayer meetings or otherwise, partly reflected the fact that if God's will could be identified (a notoriously difficult matter) this could provide a basis for unity, and it could at least be hoped that God would guide people through prayer to what he wanted. There was not a conscious search for compromise as such, and still less a desire to settle matters by majority voting, but there is clear evidence of participants listening to each other and rethinking their positions, as on the franchise.

From the point of view of unity, the recorded Debates were a failure. For this there were three main reasons. One was the *Agreement* itself, which proposed a settlement on a wholly different basis from the one the Army was already committed to. The second was the presence of civilians, not involved in the Army's previous engagements, not having the same need for unity in the Army and (at least in Wildman's case) wholly committed to their own proposals. The third was Rainborough, pursuing his quarrel with Cromwell. The dismay of other participants about the sometimes bad-tempered debate and the lack of progress towards agreement is clear from much of the transcript.

Another thing to remember in reading the Debates is the sense of being beset by dangers − from the Presbyterians, from the King still seeking to raise new armies, from division within the Army, from growing splits among Independents both in Parliament and the Army about whether there should be further negotiations with the King, and from a population infuriated by the continuing high taxes and centralised authority. The Army had survived in 1647 only though a series of extraordinary events. Those at Putney did not know that it would eventually take even more power to itself in 1648-9 and resolve the problem of the Parliament by drastically purging it and of the King by executing him. At least as likely was that the Army would be overthrown by disunity, by risings of its many enemies or by a peace settlement which failed to provide adequately for indemnity or restored too much power to the King. This could endanger not only what they had fought for but also their lives; the several references to the possibility of the King executing them were no mere rhetorical flourishes. The King is ever-present in the recorded Debates at Putney.

There was consequently a strong motivation to agree on proposals which could form the basis of a satisfactory settlement. The Debates were not an academic discussion but were intended to result in peace proposals which could actually be implemented.

Day 1: 28 October 1647

The Debates began with Sexby, apparently speaking on behalf of the new agents, bluntly putting the case that Cromwell and Ireton had lost credit because of their attempts to reach agreement with the King and establish good relations with Parliament. After Cromwell and Ireton had answered this charge (apparently convincingly), the *Agreement* was read. Cromwell made three points against it, setting the terms of the debate for much of the first day. First, it would make very radical changes, raising the prospect of anarchy. Secondly, he asked what would happen if an Agreement based on the sovereignty of the people was not agreed to by the people. Thirdly he raised the question of whether the proposed new constitution was consistent with the engagements already entered into by the Army. Much of the first day was concerned with the circumstances in which it was acceptable to break an engagement. Towards the end of the day Cromwell made his famous remark that he was not 'wedded and glued to forms of government'.

Sexby's opening remarks highlighted the issue of negotiations with the King. Whereas there had been much goodwill in the Army towards the King earlier in 1647, this had diminished as he proved evasive in negotiations. It was the future of the King – whether negotiations should continue with him, whether any of his power could safely be restored and whether he should be punished in some way – rather than the franchise which was the most divisive issue at Putney, dividing all ranks rather than setting officers against men.

According to a newspaper, the meeting continued 'from morning untill night'. There were two outcomes. Following an emotional appeal by Goffe, it was agreed to devote the following morning to prayer in order to seek God's will. It was also agreed to establish a committee (including many radical members) to review the *Agreement* in the light of the Army's engagements.

At the General Council of Officers at Putney.

Cromwell: That the meeting was for public businesses. Those that had anything to say concerning the public business might have liberty to speak.

Sexby: We have been by providence put upon strange things, such as the ancientest here doth scarce remember. The Kingdom's cause requires expedition, and truly our miseries with those of our fellow soldiers cry out for present help. The cause of our misery is upon two things. We sought to satisfy all men, and it was well; but in going about to do it we have dissatisfied all men. We have laboured to please a King, and I think, except we go about to cut all our throats, we shall not please him; and we have gone to support a house which will prove rotten studs, I mean the Parliament which consists of a company of rotten Members. I shall

Fig. 17. Henry Ireton (1611-51), Commissary-General – second in command of the cavalry under Cromwell. (Portrait by Robert Walker.) Ireton was the main speaker against a wider franchise at the Putney Debates.

speak to the Lieutenant General and Commissary General concerning one thing: your credits and reputation hath been much blasted upon these two considerations. I desire you will consider those things that shall be offered to you; and if you see anything of reason, you will join with us that the Kingdom may be eased, and our fellow soldiers may be quieted in spirit.

Cromwell: I dare avow I have acted nothing but what I have done with the public consent and approbation and allowance of the General Council. What I have spoken in another capacity, as a Member of the House, that was free for me to do.

Ireton: I do detest and defy the thought of that thing, of any endeavour, or design, or purpose, or desire to set up the King. Yet I shall declare it again, I do not seek, or would not seek, nor will join with them that do seek the destruction either of Parliament or King.

[*The answer of the new agents was read by William Allen.*]

Ireton: By this paper they seem to be of a fixed resolution, setting themselves to be a divided party or a distinct council from the General Council of the Army. The gentlemen that brought that paper have been since induced to descend a little from the heights, and to send some of them to come as agents or messengers.

Buff-Coat [Everard]: [We believe that] according to my expectations and your engagement you are resolved every one to purchase our inheritances which have been lost, and free this nation from the tyranny that lies upon us. I question not but that it is all your desires. We have here met on purpose according to my engagement that whatsoever may be thought to be necessary for our satisfaction, for the right understanding one of another [may be done] that we might go on together.

[*The* Agreement *was read.*]

Cromwell: Truly this paper does contain in it very great alterations of the very government of the Kingdom, alterations from that government that it hath been under, I believe I may almost say since it was a nation. Although the pretensions in it and the expressions in it are very plausible, how do we know if whilst we are disputing these things another company of men shall gather together, and they shall put out a paper as plausible perhaps as this? And not only another, and another, but many of this kind. And if so, what do you think the consequence of that would be? Would it not be utter confusion? Would it not make England like the Switzerland country, one canton of the Swiss against another, and one county against another? And if so, what would that produce but an absolute desolation – an absolute desolation to the nation – and we in the meantime tell the nation, "It is for your liberty, 'tis for your privilege", " 'tis for your good". Pray God it prove so whatsoever course we run.

But truly, I think we are not only to consider what the consequences are but the probability of the ways and means to accomplish it: that is to say whether, according to reason and judgment, the spirits and temper of the people of this nation are prepared to receive and to go on along with it. There will be very great mountains in the way of this. It is not enough to propose things that are good in the end, but suppose this model were an excellent model, and fit for England and the Kingdom to receive, it is our duty as Christians and men to consider consequences.

We have in the time of our danger issued out declarations; we have been required by the Parliament, because our declarations were general, to declare particularly what we meant; and having done that how far that obliges or not obliges us, that is by us to be considered, if we mean honestly and sincerely and to approve ourselves to God as honest men. He that departs from that that is a real engagement and a real tie upon him, I think he transgresses without faith. Before we take [your paper] into consideration, it is fit for us to consider how far we are obliged, and how far we are free; and I hope we shall prove ourselves honest men where we are free to tender anything to the good of the public.

Wildman: Whatever obligation is past must be considered afterwards, when it is urged whether it were honest or just or no; and if it were not just it doth not oblige the persons, [even] if it be an oath itself. By the consideration of the justice of what is offered that obligation shall appear whether it was just or no.

Ireton: This is a principle that will take away all Commonwealths, and will take away the fruit of this engagement [*the* Agreement] if it were entered into; and men of this principle would think themselves as little [obliged] as may be if in their apprehensions it be not a good law. I confess there are plausible things in [the paper], and there are things really good in it, and there are those things that I do with my heart desire. But truly I do account we are under engagements; we who are the Army and are engaged with public declarations [should] consider how far those public declarations, which we then thought to be just, do oblige, that we may either resolve to make them good if we can in honest ways, or at least not make it our work to break them.

Rainborough: There are two objections are made against [the paper]. The one is division. Truly I think we are utterly undone if we divide, but I hope that honest things have carried us on thus long, and will keep us together, and I hope that we shall not divide.

31

Another thing is difficulties. Oh unhappy men are we that ever began this war; if ever we had looked upon difficulties I do not know that ever we should have looked an enemy in the face. Truly I think the parliament were very indiscreet to contest with the King if they did not consider first that they should go through difficulties. Let the difficulties be round about you, have you death before you, the sea on each side of you and behind you, are you convinced that the thing is just, I think you are bound in conscience to carry it on.

I hear it said, "It's a huge alteration, it's a bringing in of new laws", and that this Kingdom hath been under this government ever since it was a Kingdom. If writings be true there hath been many scufflings between the honest men of England and those that have tyrannised over them. If [the laws] were those which the people have been always under, if the people find that they are not suitable to freemen as they are, I know no reason should deter me, either in what I must answer before God or the world, from endeavouring by all means to gain anything that might be of more advantage to them than the Government under which they live. All that is to be considered is the justness of the thing.

Cromwell: I do not think that it was at all offered by anybody that though an engagement were never so unrighteous it ought to be kept. For certainly it's an act of duty to break an unrighteous engagement. But this was only offered, that before we can consider of this paper we labour to know where we are, and where we stand. Perhaps we are upon engagements that we cannot with honesty break, but let me tell you this, that he that speaks to you of engagements here is as free from engagements to the King as any man in all the world. Our engagements are public engagements; they are to the Kingdom.

I shall move that we may have a committee amongst ourselves to consider of the engagements, and this committee to dispute things with others. I doubt not but if in sincerity we are willing to submit to that light that God shall cast in among us God will unite us. I shall desire this, that you or any other of the agitators or gentlemen that can be here will be here, that we may have free discourses amongst ourselves of things, and you will be able to satisfy each other.

Bedfordshire man: I confess my ignorance in those engagements, but I apprehend, at least I hope, that those engagements have given away nothing from the people that is the people's right. It may be they have promised the King his right, or any other persons their right, but no more. If they have promised more than their right to any person or persons, and have given away anything from the people that is their right, then I conceive they are unjust. I conceive that for the substance of the paper it is the people's due; and for the change of the government which is so dangerous, I apprehend that there may be many dangers in it, and truly I apprehend there may be more dangers without it. For I conceive if you keep the government as it is and bring in the King, there may be more dangers than in changing the government. And I shall desire that those that conceive themselves bound up would desist, and be no hindrances to hinder the people.

Goffe: The motion is that there might be a seeking of God in the things that now lie before us. Since there are so many of us that have had so many and so large experiences of an extraordinary manifestation of God's presence, when we have been in such extraordinary ways met together, I shall desire that those who are that way inclined will take the present opportunity to do it. There have been those that have preached to us in this place that God would be with us no longer than we were with him. We have in some things wandered from God. Let us not be ashamed to declare

Fig. 18. Lieutenant-Colonel William Goffe, the most overtly religious speaker at the Putney Debates.

to all the world that our counsels, and our wisdom, and our ways they are not altogether such as the world hath walked in, but that we have had a dependency upon God, and that our desires are to follow God if God may have the glory by it. And I pray let us consider this: God does seem evidently to be throwing down the glory of all flesh; the greatest powers in the Kingdom have been shaken. God hath thrown down the glory of the King and that party; he hath thrown down a party in the City; I do not say that God will throw us down – I hope better things – but he will have the glory; let us not stand upon our glory and reputation in the world. I hope our strayings from God are not so great, but that a conversion and true humiliation may recover us again.

Cromwell: For my part I shall lay aside all business for this business, either to convince or be convinced as God shall please. I think it would be good that tomorrow morning may be spent in prayer, and the afternoon might be the time of our business.

Ireton: That which Lieut. Col. Goffe offered hath made a very great impression upon me. He hath never spoke but he hath touched my heart. In the time of our straits and difficulties, I think we none of us – I am sure I have not – walked so closely with God, and kept so close with him, as to trust wholly upon him, as not to be led too much with considerations of danger and difficulty.

[*The prayer meeting was agreed to, but Petty and Everard indicated that they could not themselves make new commitments on behalf of those who had sent them.*]

Wildman: [There] is a principle much spreading and much to my trouble, and that is this: that when persons once be engaged, though the engagement appear to be unjust, yet the person must set down and suffer under it; and that therefore, in case a Parliament, as a true Parliament, doth anything unjustly, if we be engaged to submit to the laws that they shall make, if they make an unjust law, though they make an unrighteous law, yet we must swear obedience. Whereas it is contrary to what the Army first declared: that they stood upon such principles of right and freedom, and the laws of nature and nations, whereby men were to preserve themselves though the persons to whom authority belonged should fail in it. The necessity of the Kingdom for present actings is such that two or three days may lose the Kingdom; I mean there may be an agreement between the King [and the Parliament]. Whereas it is desired that engagements may be considered, I shall desire that only the justice of the thing that is proposed may be considered. Whether the chief thing in the Agreement, the intent of it, be not this, to secure the rights of the people in their Parliaments, which was declared by this Army in the Declaration of the 14th of June to be absolutely insisted on?

Ireton: I am far from holding that if a man have engaged himself to a thing that is not just – to a thing that is evil, that is sin if he do it – that that man is still bound to perform what he hath promised. But when we talk of just, it is not so much of what is sinful before God, but it intends of that which is just according to the foundation of justice between man and man. There is no other foundation of right I know of but this general justice, and this general ground of righteousness, that we should keep covenant one with another. I would very fain know what you gentlemen or any other do account the right you have to anything in England, anything of estate, land or goods that you have? What right hath any man to anything if you lay not that principle, that we are to keep covenant? If you will resort only to the law of nature, by the law of nature you have no more right to this land or anything else than I have. And therefore when I hear men speak of laying aside all engagements to consider only that wild or vast notion of what in every man's conception is just or unjust, I am afraid and do tremble at the boundless and endless consequences of it.

Wildman: Our sense was that an unjust engagement is rather to be broken than kept. I do apply this to the case in hand: that it might be considered whether it be unjust to bring in the King in such a way as he may be in a capacity to destroy the people.

Ireton: Whatsoever we have declared in the Army declarations it is no more but this. The Parliament hath commanded us to do this. We have said no. First we have insisted upon the fundamental rights of the people. We have said we desire first to have the constitution of the supreme authority of this Kingdom reduced to that constitution which is due to the people of this Kingdom, and reducing the authority to this we will submit to it, we will acquiesce, we will cast our share into this common bottom.

Cromwell: If any come to us tomorrow only to instruct us and teach us, how far that will consist with the liberty of a free debate or an end of satisfaction I refer to every sober-spirited man to think of and determine. If we may come to an honest and single debate, we shall meet with a great deal the more comfort, and hopes of a good and happy issue. But if otherwise, I despair of the meeting; or at least I would have the meeting to be of another notion, a meeting that did represent the agitators of five regiments to give rules to the Council of War. We shall meet to prejudice – really to the prejudice of the Kingdom, and of the whole Army – if we be thus absolutely resolved upon our way and engaged beforehand.

The Kingdom will see it is such a real actual division as admits of no reconciliation.

Rainborough: Not that the engagements of the Army are looked upon as destructive, but the not-performance of the engagements of the Army is that which is destructive.

Lockyer: I have gathered from two men's mouths that destruction is something near, and the cause of the destruction as they understand is the going of the proposals to the King. I think it were very necessary that if it be true, as is supposed, the proposals may be brought hither when they do go, that we may see what they are.

Merriman: You have both promised to free the people, which you may do by taking off tithes and other antichristian yokes upon them, and to give contents to the soldiers.

Cromwell: Really I am persuaded in my conscience it is their aim [*the new agents and their friends*] to act as may be most for the good of the people. Now if that be in your spirits and our spirits, it remains only that God show us the way and lead us in the way, which I hope he will. There may be some prejudices upon some of your spirits that we are wedded and glued to forms of government, so that whatsoever we may pretend, it is in vain for you to speak to us or to hope for any agreement from us. You will find that we are far from being so particularly engaged to anything to the prejudice of this – further than the notorious engagements that the world takes notice of – that we should not concur with you that the foundation and supremacy is in the people, radically in them.

Day 2: 29 October 1647

This is the famous day of the Debates, when the franchise was debated and Rainborough made his remark about 'the poorest he'. It is the reason why the Debates are still commemorated. However, it was not a formal meeting of the General Council and it did not take place in the church. The prayer meeting agreed the previous day was at Mr Chamberlain's, a house on the east side of the High Street which stood until 1872. The transcript covers the last stages of the prayer meeting and then moves without a break into the afternoon's discussion (at 1 or 2 o'clock), with the new agent, Everard, speaking and Cromwell asking if 'those gentlemen that are now come would draw nigher'. The transcript occasionally hints at what must have been a crowded room, with people sitting in every available space. Cromwell referred to Everard as 'my friend at my back', and Colonel Rich was described as 'the gentleman in the window', as was William Allen.

The length of the prayer meeting had left no time for the committee on the Army's engagements to meet. Cromwell considered (rightly) that it would be more productive if the committee first met the new agents and their friends and then the General Council met in the evening, rather than a very large meeting having an unstructured discussion on the *Agreement* immediately, but he eventually gave way. He and Ireton would have been in a much stronger position if consensus had first been achieved on the Army's engagements.

The clerk read out the *Agreement*, and debate began on its first clause. This called for representation in the Commons to be more equal, as the Army had itself called for, but instead of the Army's proposal of representation being proportional to taxation, it was to be 'according to the number of the inhabitants'. Ireton immediately attacked this as implying that every man was to have an equal vote. In a debate dominated by four people – Ireton and Cromwell on one side and Rainborough and Wildman on the other – both sides took up extreme positions. Ireton argued that only landowners and members of corporations (those with 'a permanent fixed interest in this Kingdom') should have the vote. This would have been a much narrower franchise than the existing one. There was a property qualification for county constituencies – the 40 shilling freehold – but this was not always enforced, and many boroughs had a franchise which in practice included all male householders. In fact Ireton conceded that he was willing to see some expansion of the franchise provided it was not 'beyond all bounds'. He found little support for his restrictive view.

On the other side, Rainborough argued that no-one was bound to obey a Government he had had no voice in placing himself under. Both Rainborough and Sexby asked what the ordinary soldiers had fought for if simply to make themselves slaves to the rich, receiving the answer that they had fought to curb royal absolutism. No-one suggested giving the vote to women as well as men.

The deep and ill-tempered disagreement, and the length of the debate upon just

Figs. 19 and 20 (left). Thomas Chamberlain's house, where the debate on the franchise took place, as it looked shortly before its demolition in 1872. It was built by John Parr, embroiderer, in the 1590s, and was known as the White House. In the eighteenth century it was re-faced with sash windows, as shown here. Sainsbury's supermarket now stands on its garden. Why it was favoured for meetings in 1647 is unknown; perhaps it had an unusually large room, such as a long gallery, as the second-floor windows at the back suggest.

one point in the *Agreement*, evidently caused dismay, and Cromwell and others moved towards compromise. Even Petty agreed that apprentices, servants and those receiving alms should be excluded, 'because they depend on the will of other men' and therefore could not vote freely (no-one had the idea of a secret ballot).

Just when a consensus seemed within reach, Rainborough called for a general rendezvous of the Army, which he presumably expected to endorse the *Agreement*. He was implying that the officers had reneged on the commitment that the Army would not divide or disband until its grievances were satisfied. The remainder of the discussion dealt with the Army's engagements, whether the *Agreement* really went much further than the Army had already demanded and whether the King and House of Lords should continue to be able to block laws passed by the Commons. The transcript breaks off inconclusively.

The debate on the franchise has many ironies. As the *Agreement* did not specifically mention the franchise, the debate could have moved on to matters on which agreement was more likely if Ireton had not raised it. If he had not raised it in the particular way that he did, putting an extreme case, debate might have concentrated on the detail of who the franchise should be extended to, rather than becoming a discussion about the principles, which is what makes it so exciting to read. Although it was a controversial issue, there was scope for compromise, as eventually emerged; indeed it is not clear that the Levellers had fully thought through their ideas on the franchise, or taken account of the fact that a wide franchise would probably have produced a royalist Parliament. Moreover, judging by their later activities, the franchise was not one of the things the Levellers cared most deeply about, and the same was true of the ordinary soldiers. But the greatest irony is that agreement *was* in fact reached. Although the transcript does not record it, two other sources indicate that before the meeting ended the General Council agree to extend the vote to 'all souldiers and others, if they be not servants or beggars', with only three or four votes against. Had this been implemented, the country's political life would have been transformed.

At the meeting of the officers for calling upon God.

Goffe: Let us inquire whether some of the actions that we have done of late do not cross the work of God in these particulars; because in our proposing things we do endeavour to set up that power which God would not set up again. I mean in our compliance with that party [*the King*] which God hath engaged us to destroy.

I desire to speak something that may concern some persons that may stand, or at least may seem to stand, in direct opposition to us; and truly I wish we may be very wary what we do, and let us take heed of rejecting any of the saints of God before God rejects them.

Everard: This honourable Council hath given me great encouragement. Though I have many impediments in my speech, yet I thank you that you will hear me speak. Our desires are nothing but to follow our work to deliver the Kingdom from that burden that lies upon us. For my part I am but a poor man and unacquainted with the affairs of the Kingdom, yet this message God hath sent me to you, that there is great expectation of sudden destruction. We desire your joint consent to seek out some speedy way for the relief of the Kingdom.

[*Cromwell proposed that the committee on engagements should meet first, so as to prepare well for a wider meeting in the evening or the following day, but this was not agreed.*]

Ireton: Neither do I care for the engagements of the Army so much for the engagements' sake, but I look upon this Army as having carried with it hitherto the name of God. The name and honour of God, the name and reputation of the people of God, and of that Gospel that they profess, is deeply and dearly and nearly concerned in the good or ill manage of this Army, and therefore for my part I profess it, that's the only thing to me. It is not to me so much as the vainest or lightest thing you can imagine, whether there be a King in England or no, or whether there be Lords in England or no. For whatever I find the work of God tending to I should desire quietly to submit to. If God saw it good to destroy, not only King and Lords, but all distinctions of degrees – nay if it go further, to destroy all property, that there's no such thing left, that there be nothing at all of civil constitution left in the Kingdom – if I see the hand of God in it I hope I shall with quietness acquiesce and submit to it, and not resist it. But still I think that God certainly will so lead this Army that they may not incur sin, or bring scandal upon the name of God, and the name of the people of God that are both so nearly concerned in what this Army does. And therefore it is my wish that we consider first engagements. I would not have us to give the world occasion to think that we are the disturbers of the peace of mankind.

[*However, Ireton conceded that the* Agreement *should be read and considered both on its merits and in relation to the Army's engagements. The* Agreement *was read in full, and then its first article, which provided that representation in Parliament should be in proportion to population.*]

Ireton: This doth make me think that the meaning is that every man that is an inhabitant is to be equally considered, and to have an equal voice in the election of the representors; and if that be the meaning then I have something to say against it.   If it be intended that those that by that constitution that was before the Conquest, that hath been beyond memory, such persons that hath been by that constitution the electors should still be the electors, I have no more to say against it.

Petty: We judge that all inhabitants that have not lost their birthright should have an equal voice in elections.

Rainborough: Really I think that the poorest he that is in England hath a life to live as the greatest he; and therefore truly, Sir, I think it's clear that every man that is to live under a Government ought first by his own consent to put himself under that Government; and I do think that the poorest man in England is not at all bound in a strict sense to that Government that he hath not had a voice to put himself under; and I am confident that when I have heard the reasons against it, something will be said to answer those reasons, in so much that I should doubt whether he was an Englishman or no that should doubt of these things.

Ireton: If you make this the rule I think you must fly for refuge to an absolute natural right, and you must deny all civil right. For my part I think it is no right at all. I think that no person hath a right to an interest or share in the disposing or determining of the affairs of the Kingdom, and in choosing those that shall determine what laws we shall be ruled by here, no person hath a right to this, that hath not a permanent fixed interest in this Kingdom; and those persons together are properly the represented of this Kingdom, and consequently are to make up the representors of this Kingdom, who taken together do comprehend whatsoever is of real or permanent interest in the Kingdom.   And I am sure I cannot tell why [otherwise] a foreigner coming in amongst us should not as well lay claim to it as any other.

We talk of birthright. Men may justly have by birthright, by their very being born in England, that we should not seclude them out of England, that we should not refuse to give them air and place and ground, and the freedom of the highways and other things, to live amongst us, not to any man that is born here, though by his birth there come nothing at all to him that is part of the permanent interest of this Kingdom. But that by a man's being born here he shall have a share in that power that shall dispose of the lands here,

Fig. 21. Colonel Thomas Rainborough, the most memorable advocate of a wider franchise at the Putney Debates. (Drawing made from a now lost painting.)

and of all things here, I do not think it a sufficient ground. Those that choose the representors for the making of laws by which this State and Kingdom are to be governed are the persons who taken together do comprehend the local interest of this Kingdom; that is, the persons in whom all land lies, and those in Corporations in whom all trading lies.

This is the most fundamental constitution of this Kingdom, which if you do not allow you allow none at all. If we shall go to take away this fundamental part of the civil constitution we shall plainly go to take away all property and interest that any man hath, either in land by inheritance, or in estate by possession, or anything else. If I will desire as a stranger, or claim as one freeborn here, the air, the free passage of highways, the protection of laws and all such things, if I will either desire them or claim them, I (if I have no permanent interest in that Kingdom) must submit to those laws and those rules which those shall choose who taken together do comprehend the whole interest of the Kingdom.

Rainborough: I do think that the main cause why Almighty God gave men reason, it was that they should make use of that reason, and that they should improve it for that end and purpose [*choosing representatives*] that God gave it them. I think there is nothing that God hath given a man that anyone else can take from him. Therefore I say that either it must be the law of God or the law of man that must prohibit the meanest man in the Kingdom to have this benefit as well as the greatest. I do not find anything in the law of God that a Lord shall choose 20 burgesses and a gentleman but two, or a poor man shall choose none. I find no such thing in the law of nature, nor in the law of nations. But I do find, that all Englishmen must be subject to English laws, and I do verily believe that there is no man but will say that the foundation of all law lies in the people, and if it lie in the people I am to seek for this exemption [from the right to vote].

Many a man whose zeal and affection to God and this Kingdom hath carried him forth in this cause [*for Parliament*] hath so spent his estate that in the way the State, the Army are going he shall not hold up his head; and when his estate is lost, and not worth 40s. a year, a man shall not have any interest; and there are many other ways by which estates men have do fall to decay, if that be the rule which God in his providence does use. A man when he hath an estate hath an interest in making laws; when he hath none, he hath no power in it. So that a man cannot lose that which he hath for the maintenance of his family, but he must [also] lose that which God and nature hath given him. Therefore I am still of the

43

same opinion, that every man born in England cannot, ought not, neither by the law of God nor the law of nature, to be exempted from the choice of those who are to make laws for him to live under, and for him, for aught I know, to lose his life under. Therefore I think there can be no great stick in this.

As for this of corporations it is as contrary to freedom as may be. For Sir, what is it? The King he grants a patent under the Broad-seal of England to such a corporation to send burgesses [to Parliament]. When a poor base corporation from the King's grant shall send two burgesses, when 500 men of estate shall not send one, when those that are to make their laws are called by the King, or cannot act but by such a call, truly I think that the people of England have little freedom.

Ireton: I think I agreed to this matter, that all should be equally distributed. But the question is, whether it should be distributed to all persons, or whether the same persons that are the electors now should be the electors still, and it be equally distributed amongst them. I do not see anybody else that makes this objection, and if nobody else be sensible of it I shall soon have done. All the main thing that I speak for is because I would have an eye to property. For here is the case of the most fundamental part of the constitution of the Kingdom, which if you take away, you take away all by that. Here are men of this and this quality are determined to be the electors of men to Parliament, and they are all those who have any permanent interest in the Kingdom, and who taken together do comprehend the whole interest of the Kingdom. I mean by permanent, local, that is not anywhere else. As for instance, he that hath a freehold, and that freehold cannot be removed out of the Kingdom. He that hath his livelihood by his trade, and by his freedom of trading in such a corporation which he cannot exercise in another, he is tied to that place, his livelihood depends upon it. That man hath an interest, hath a permanent interest there, upon which he may live, and live a freeman without dependence.

Now I wish we may all consider of what right you will challenge, that all the people should have right to elections. Is it by the right of nature? If you will hold forth that as your ground, then I think you must deny all property too, and this is my reason. For thus: by that same right of nature, whatever it be that you pretend, by which you can say, "one man hath an equal right with another to the choosing of him that shall govern him" – by the same right of nature, he hath an equal right in any goods he sees: meat, drink, clothes, to take and use them for his sustenance. He hath the same freedom to anything that anyone doth account himself to have any propriety in. Possibly [he] may not have so real a regard to the peace of the Kingdom as that man who hath a permanent interest in it. He that is here today and gone tomorrow, I do not see that he hath such a permanent interest.

Rainborough: If I have no interest in the Kingdom I must suffer by all their laws be they right or wrong. I am a poor man, therefore I must be pressed. Nay thus: a gentleman lives in a country and hath three or four lordships as some men hath – God knows how they got them – and when a Parliament is called he must be a Parliament man; and it may be he sees some poor men, they live near this man, he can crush them.

God hath set down that thing as to propriety with this law of his, "Thou shalt not steal". I wish you would not make the world believe that we are for anarchy.

Cromwell: No man says that you have a mind to anarchy, but the consequence of this rule tends to anarchy, must end in anarchy; for where is there any bound or limit set if you take away this limit, that men that have no interest but the interest of breathing shall have no voices in elections. Therefore I am confident on it we should not be so hot one with another.

Ireton: It is said that there is no law, no divine law, that tells us that such a corporation must have the election of burgesses, or such a shire, or the like. Our property as well as our right of sending burgesses descends from other things. That divine law does not determine particulars but generals.

Rainborough: I would fain know how [the franchise] comes to be the property [of some men and not of others]; I deny that that is a property to a Lord, to a gentleman, to any man more than another in the Kingdom of England. If it be a property, it is a property by a law; I think that the law of the land in that thing is the most tyrannical law under heaven, and I would fain know what we have fought for, and this is the old law of England and that which enslaves the people of England, that they should be bound by laws in which they have no voice at all.

Petty: As for this argument that it destroys all right to property that every Englishman that is an inhabitant of England should choose and have a choice in the representatives, I suppose it is [on the contrary] the only means to preserve all property. For I judge every man is naturally free; and I judge the reason why men when they were in so great numbers [chose representatives was] that every man could not give his voice; and therefore men agreed to come into some form of Government that they who were chosen might preserve property.

Ireton: If I had said that I would not wish that we should have any enlargement at all of the bounds of those that are to be the electors, then you might have excepted against it. But what I said was that I would not go to enlarge it beyond all bounds: that upon the same ground you may admit of so many men from foreign states as would outvote you. I do not mean that I would have it restrained to that proportion it is now, but to restrain it still to men who have a local, a permanent interest in the Kingdom, who have such an interest that they may live upon it as freemen, and who have such an interest as is fixed upon a place, and is not the same everywhere equally. If a man be an inhabitant upon a rack rent for a year, for two years, or 20 years – you cannot think that man hath any fixed or permanent interest – that man if he pay the rent that his land is worth, and hath no advantage but what he hath by his land, that man is as good a man, may have as much interest in another Kingdom as here. If you go beyond this law, if you admit any man that hath a breath and being, it may come to destroy property thus: you may have such men chosen or at least the major part of them [as have no local and permanent interest]. Why may not those men vote against all property? You may admit strangers by this rule, if you admit them once to inhabit, and those that have interest in the land may be voted out of their land. Show me why you will not, by the same right of nature, make use of anything that any man hath necessary for the sustenance of men. Show me what you will stop at.

Rainborough: I desire to know how this comes to be a property in some men and not in others.

Rich: I confess there is weight in that objection that the Commissary General [*Ireton*] last insisted upon: for you have five to one in this Kingdom that have no permanent interest. Some men have ten, some twenty servants, some more, some less. If the master and servant shall be equal electors, then clearly those that have no interest in the Kingdom will make it their interest to choose those that have no interest. It may happen that the majority may by law, not in a confusion, destroy property; there may be a law enacted that there shall be an equality of goods and estate. But there may be a more equal division and distribution than that he that hath nothing should have an equal voice; and certainly there may be some other way thought of that there may be a representative of the poor as well as the rich, and not to exclude all. I remember there were as we have heard many workings and revolutions in the Roman Senate [under] this kind of distribution of election; that the people's voices were bought and sold, and that by the poor, and thence it came that he that was the richest man made himself a perpetual dictator.

Wildman: Our case is to be considered thus, that we have been under slavery. That's acknowledged by all. Our very laws were made by our conquerors; and whereas it's spoken much of chronicles, I conceive there is no credit to be given to any of them; and the reason is because those that were our Lords, and made us their vassals, would suffer nothing else to be chronicled. We are now engaged for our freedom. Every person in England hath as clear a right to elect his representative as the greatest person in England. I conceive that's the undeniable maxim of government: that all government is in the free consent of the people. If the question be stated, it might rather be this: whether any person can justly be bound by law, who doth not give his consent that such persons shall make laws for him?

Ireton: If a foreigner come within this Kingdom, this man ought to be subject to those laws, and to be bound by those laws so long as he continues amongst them, though neither he nor his ancestors, not any betwixt him and Adam, did ever give concurrence to this constitution. If this man do think himself unsatisfied to be subject to this law he may go into another kingdom. And so the same reason doth extend in my understanding to that man that hath no permanent interest in the Kingdom. If he hath money, his money is as good in another place as here; he hath nothing that doth locally fix him to this Kingdom. If this man will live in this Kingdom or trade among us, that man ought to subject himself to the law made by the people who have the interest of this Kingdom in us.

William Rainborough: I think if it can be made to appear that it is a just and reasonable thing, and that it is for the preservation of all the freeborn men, it ought to be made good unto them. The reason is that the chief end of this Government is to preserve persons as well as estates, and if any law shall take hold of my person it is more dear than my estate.

Rainborough: I do not hear any argument given but only that it is the present law of the Kingdom. I say still, what shall become of those many men that have laid out themselves for the Parliament of England in this present war, that have ruined themselves by fighting, by hazarding all they had?

Ireton: The law of God doth not give me property, nor the law of nature, but property is of humane constitution. Constitution founds property. Though I shall acquiesce in having no property, yet I cannot give my heart or hand to it; because it is a thing evil in itself and scandalous to the world, and I desire this Army may be free from both.

Sexby: We have engaged in this Kingdom and ventured our lives, and it was all for this: to recover our birthrights and privileges as Englishmen, and by the arguments urged there is none. There are many thousands of us soldiers that have ventured our lives; we have had little propriety in the Kingdom as to our estates, yet we have had a birthright. But it seems now except a man hath a fixed estate in this Kingdom, he hath no right in this Kingdom. I wonder we were so much deceived. If we had not a right to the Kingdom, we were mere mercenary soldiers. I am resolved to give my birthright to none. I do think the poor and meaner of this Kingdom have been the means of the preservation of this Kingdom.

Ireton: If a man mean by birthright, whatsoever he can challenge by the law of nature, suppose there were no constitution at all, supposing no civil law and civil constitution, you leave no property, nor any foundation for any man to enjoy anything.

Rainborough: Sir, I see that it is impossible to have liberty but all property must be taken away. If it be laid down for a rule, and if you will say it, it must be so. But I would fain know what the soldier hath fought for all this while? He hath fought to enslave himself, to give power to men of riches, men of estates, to make him a perpetual slave. We do find in all presses that go forth none must be pressed that are freehold men. When these gentlemen fall out among themselves they shall press the poor scrubs to come and kill them.

Ireton: I tell you what the soldier of the Kingdom hath fought for. The danger that we stood in was, that one man's will must be a law; that is, that the will of one man should not be a law, but that the law of this Kingdom should be by a choice of persons to represent, and that choice to be made by the generality of the Kingdom. Here was a right that induced men to fight. Liberty may be had and property not be destroyed.

[*Mr Peter apparently proposed that all those who had fought for Parliament should have votes.*]

Cromwell: I confess I was most dissatisfied with that I heard Mr Sexby speak of any man here, because it did savour so much of will. Everybody here would be willing that the representative might be mended, that is, it might be better than it is. Perhaps there are a very considerable part of copyholders by inheritance that ought to have a voice. I think if you do desire to bring this to a result it were well if we may but resolve upon a committee.

Sexby: I am sorry that my zeal to what I apprehend is good should be so ill resented. Do you not think it were a sad and miserable condition that we have fought all this time for nothing? All here both great and small do think that we fought for something. I confess many of us fought for those ends which we since saw was not that which caused us to go through difficulties and straits to venture all in the ship with you. It had been good in you to have advertised us of it, and I believe you would have fewer under your command to be commanded.

I think there are many that have not estates that in honesty have as much right in the freedom of their choice as any that have great estates. Truly Sir, as for your putting off this question and coming to some other, I dare say that they cannot settle upon any other until this be done. It was the ground that we took up arms, and it is the ground which we shall maintain. Concerning my making rents and divisions in this way, as a particular, if I were but so, I could lie down and be trodden there; but truly I am sent by a regiment; if I should not speak, guilt shall lie upon me.

Ireton: I will ask that gentleman that spoke, whom I love in my heart, whether when they drew out to serve the Parliament in the beginning, when they engaged with the Army at Newmarket [*in June 1647*], whether then they thought of any more interest or right in the Kingdom than this? Whether they did think that they should have as great interest in Parliament men as freeholders had? Or whether from the beginning we did not engage for the liberty of parliaments, and that we should be [bound] by the laws that such did make. If you will appoint a committee to consider of some of that, so as you preserve the equitable part of that, who are like to be freemen, and men not given up to the wills of others, I will go with you as far as I can.

Rolfe: I shall desire that there may be some thoughts of a medium or a composure, in relation to servants or to foreigners, or such others as shall be agreed upon.

Chillenden: If we take this course of debating upon one question a whole afternoon, if the danger be so near as it is supposed, it were the ready way to bring us into it.

Clarke: I presume that all people and all nations whatsoever have a liberty and power to alter and change their constitutions, if they find them to be weak and infirm. Now if the people of England shall find this weakness in their constitution, they may change it if they please.

Audley: I would die in any place in England in asserting that it is the right of every freeborn man to elect, according to the rule, that which concerns all ought to be debated by all.

Ireton: If there be anything at all that is a foundation of liberty it is this, that those who shall choose the lawmakers shall be men freed from dependence upon others. That liberty which we so much talk of and have contended for shall be nothing at all by putting it into the hands of those men that will give it away when they have it.

Cromwell: If we should go about to alter these things, I do not think that we are bound to fight for every particular proposition. Servants while servants are not included. Then you agree that he that receives alms is to be excluded.

Reade: I see no reason why any man that is a native ought to be excluded that privilege [of choosing representatives], unless from voluntary servitude.

Petty: I conceive the reason why we would exclude apprentices, or servants, or those that take alms, is because they depend upon the will of other men and should be afraid to displease them.

Everard: I being sent from the agents of the five regiments with an answer unto a writing, the committee was very desirous to inquire into the depth of our intentions. It was the Lieutenant General's desire for an understanding with us, presuming those things I did declare did tend to unity, "and if so you will let it appear by coming unto us". We stand upon the principles of unity and freedom. I heard that there are meetings daily and contrivances against us. Now for our parts I hope you will not say all is yours, but we have nakedly and freely unbosomed ourselves unto you. Though those things have startled many at the first view, yet we find there is good hopes. We have fixed our resolutions, and we are determined, and we want nothing but that only God will direct us to what is just and right. But I understand that in all these debates if we shall agree upon any one thing, "this is our freedom", "this is our liberty", "this liberty and freedom we are debarred of and we are bereaved of all those comforts", in case we should find out half a hundred of these, yet the main business is how we should find them, and how we should come by them. When I heard the Lieutenant General speak I was marvellously taken up with the plainness of the carriage. I said "I will bring them to you", "you shall see if their hearts be so; for my part I see nothing but plainness and uprightness of heart made manifest unto you".

Waller: I think if we do make it our resolution that we do hold it forth to all powers, Parliament or King, or whoever they are, to let them know that these are our rights, and if we have them not, we must get them the best way we can.

Rainborough: Moved, That the Army might be called to a rendezvous, and things settled.

Ireton: We are called back to engagements. What else is there in this paper but that we have acted so vigorously for already? I say plainly the way they have taken hath been the way of disunion and division.

Agitator: Whereas you say the agents did it, it was the soldiers did put the agents upon these meetings. It was the dissatisfactions that were in the Army which provoked, which occasioned those meetings, which you suppose tends so much to dividing; and the reasons of such dissatisfactions are because those whom they had to trust to act for them were not true to them.

Ireton: There is but one thing in this [*Agreement*] that hath not been insisted upon and propounded by the Army heretofore all along [*i.e. the right of the Commons to make law without the consent of King and Lords*]. Tis true the "Proposals" said not that, and for my part, if any man will put that to the question I am in the same mind [as before, except] with that limitation that hath been all along acknowledged by the Parliament, where the safety of the Kingdom is concerned. I do agree that the King is bound by his oath at his coronation to agree to the law that the Commons shall choose without Lords or anybody else.

Petty: For my part I cannot but think that both the power of King and Lords was ever a branch of tyranny, and if ever a people shall free themselves from tyranny, certainly it is after 7 years war and fighting for their liberty. If the constitution of this Kingdom shall be established as formerly, it might rivet tyranny into this Kingdom more strongly than before.

Wildman: The agents do declare their principle, that whensoever any engagement cannot be kept justly they must break that engagement. Now though it's urged they ought to condescend to what the General Council do resolve, I conceive it's true only so long as it is for their safety. I conceive it's just and righteous for them to stand up for some more speedy vigorous actings.

I conceive it to be a very vast difference in the whole matter of proposals. The foundation of slavery was rivetted more strongly than before. As where the militia is instated in the King and Lords, and not in the Commons, there is a foundation of a future quarrel constantly laid. However, the main thing was that they found by the proposals propounded the right of the militia was acknowledged to be in the King, before any redress of any one of the people's grievances or any one of their burdens; and [the King was] so to be brought in as with a negative voice; they thought he coming in thus

51

with a negative, the Parliament are but as so many cyphers, so many round Os. They found a great uncertainty in the proposals: that they should go to the King for an act of indemnity, and thus the King might command his judges to hang them up for what they did in the wars; because the present constitution being left as it was, nothing was law but what the King signed, and not any ordinance of Parliament. And considering this, they thought it should be by an Agreement with the people, whereby a rule between the Parliament and the people might be set, so that they might be destroyed neither by the King's prerogative, nor Parliament's privileges.

Ireton: The thing then proposed [*at Reading in July*] was that we should not take away the power of the Lords in this Kingdom, and it was concluded that in the proposals. But as to the King we were clear. There is not one thing in the proposals, nor in what we declared, that doth give the King any negative voice; and therefore that's part of the scandal amongst others. We do not give the King any negative; we do but take the King as a man with whom we have been at a difference; we propound terms of peace. We do not demand that he shall have no negative, but we do not say that he shall have any.

There were many other grievances and particular matters which we did not think so necessary that they should precede the settling of a peace, which is the greatest grievance of the Kingdom. It hath been pressed by some men that we should not have subjected [our propositions] to the Parliament, but the sense of the General Council was this, that, as they had sent their propositions to the Parliament, they would see what the Parliament would do before they would conclude what themselves would do; and that there was respect [to be had] to that which we have hitherto accounted the fundamental council of the Kingdom. If all the people to a man had subscribed to this [Agreement] then there would be some security to it, because no man would oppose; but otherwise our concurrence amongst ourselves is no more than our saying ourselves we will be indemnified. I could tell you many other particulars wherein there are divers gross injuries done to the General and General Council, and such a wrong as is not fit to be done among Christians.

Day 3: 1 November 1647

A new committee, including six soldier-agitators, was appointed on 29 October to compare the Army's declarations and the *Agreement* and draw up a draft statement on what the Army should insist upon in any settlement. It met at Mr Chamberlain's house on 30 October and agreed various points, including parliaments sitting for two years, representation to be more equal on the basis of the number of electors, and the franchise to be determined by the present House of Commons, with 'as much enlargement to common freedom as may be'; there was a request to include all who had fought for or voluntarily supported Parliament in the war and to exclude at first all who had fought for the King. Continuation of the monarchy and House of Lords was tacitly assumed but with greatly reduced powers, and so was the acceptance of Parliament as the agency through which a settlement would be achieved. The committee met again on 31 October, and it was the proposals agreed then which Ireton reported to the General Council on 1 November, evidently expecting them to be welcomed.

On 1 November the main subject of debate in the General Council was the most dangerously divisive subject of all: the role of the King, and to a lesser extent the House of Lords, in any settlement, and particularly their 'negative voice' against bills passed by the Commons. Harsh language was used against the King, with Captain Bishop describing him as 'that Man of Blood'. Recent research, based on careful examination of Cromwell's words at Putney, suggests he had already decided that the King must be punished (though not necessarily executed), but that he had not yet worked out how it could be done. He did, however, make clear that if the liberty and safety of the nation required that the King be destroyed he would do it regardless of any previous engagements. Much of the day was taken up by Ireton and Wildman debating the exact significance of the King's coronation oath, and by discussion of how the will of God could be discerned.

By 1 November it was becoming clear that the Levellers were not just seeking support in the General Council through argument, but were actively encouraging soldiers to mutiny and were attempting to seize control of the Army from its senior officers. One regiment was already disobeying orders. Cromwell's warning early in this day's debate that he would maintain discipline should be seen in that context.

At the General Council of the Army.

Cromwell first moved that everyone might speak their experiences as the issue of what God had given in answer to their prayers.

Captain Allen [expressed] what experiences he had received from himself, and from divers other godly people: that the work that was before them was to take away the negative voice of the King and Lords.

Fig. 22. King Charles I. (Portrait by Daniel Mytens.)

Carter expressed his experiences; that he found not any inclination in his heart as formerly to pray for the King, that God would make him yet a blessing to the Kingdom.

Cowling: That the sword was the only thing that had from time to time recovered our rights; that our ancestors had recovered their liberties from the Danes and Normans by the sword.

Lilburne: That he never observed that the recovery of our liberties which we had before the Normans was the occasion of our taking up arms, or the main quarrel; and that the Norman laws are not slavery introduced upon us, but an augmentation of our slavery before.

54

Cromwell: I think it is their proper place to conform to the Parliament that first gave them their being. How they can take the determination of commanding men, conducting men, quartering men, keeping guards, without an authority otherwise than from themselves, I am ignorant of. Either they are a Parliament or no Parliament. If they be no Parliament they are nothing, and we are nothing likewise. The considering of what is fit for the Kingdom does belong to the Parliament.

I must confess I have a commission from the General and I understand that I am to do by it. I shall conform to him according to the rules and discipline of war; and therefore I conceive it is not in the power of any particular men or any particular man in the Army to call a rendezvous of a troop or regiment, or in the least to disoblige the Army from those commands of the General. This way is destructive to the Army and to every particular man in the Army. I have been informed by some of the King's party that if they give us rope enough we will hang ourselves.

Jubbes: Truly I do not know how to distinguish whether the spirit of God lives in me, or no, but by mercy, love and peace; and on the contrary, whether the spirit of Antichrist lives in me, but by envy, malice and war.

[*Jubbes then asked a series of questions, including: could Parliament be purged of those who had supported the Presbyterian uprising and still remain a Parliament? If it could, would the majority remedy the Army's grievances? If so, would they be willing to declare the King guilty of all the bloodshed and yet receive him as King again to avoid further wars?*]

Goffe: It was concluded by the Lieutenant-General upon what was spoken by one here, that that was not the mind of God that was spoken by him. I could wish we might be wary of such expressions. God hath spoken in several ages in sundry ways. God hath put us upon such a course which I cannot but reverence, and God does not now speak by one particular man, but in every one of our hearts; and certainly if it were a dangerous thing to refuse a message that came from one man to many, it is a more dangerous thing to refuse what comes from God, being spoke by many to us. I should add this, that it seems to me evident and clear, that this hath been a voice from heaven to us, that we have sinned against the Lord in tampering with his enemies.

Cromwell: That which he [*Gough*] speaks was that at such a meeting as this we should wait upon God. I confess it is an high duty, but when anything is spoken [as from God] I think the rule is, Let the rest judge! I do not judge conclusively, negatively, that it

55

was not of the Lord, but I do desire to submit it to all your judgments whether it was of the Lord or no. I cannot say that I have received anything that I can speak as in the name of the Lord.

William Allen: The difference between us I think is in the interest of King and Lords, some declaring against the name and title of King and Lords. According to what we have engaged we stand bound. You say you will set up the King as far as may be consistent with, and not prejudicial to, the liberties of the Kingdom; and really I am of that mind too. If the setting up of him be not consistent with them, and prejudicial to them, then down with him; but if he may be so set up – which I think he may – [then set him up], and it is not our judgement only, but that of those that set forth the Case of the Army.

Sexby: You are in a wilderness condition. We find in the word of God "I would heal Babylon, but she would not be healed". I think that we have gone about to heal Babylon when she would not. We have gone about to wash a blackamore, to wash him white, which he will not. We are going about to set up the power of Kings, some part of it, which God will destroy; and which will be but as a burthensome stone that whosoever shall fall upon it, it will destroy him.

Cromwell: I cannot but think that in most that have spoke there hath been something of God made forth to us; and yet there hath been several contradictions in what hath been spoken. But certainly God is not the author of contradictions. The contradictions are not so much in the end as in the way. The end is to deliver this nation from oppression and slavery, to accomplish that work that God hath carried us on in, to establish our hopes of justice and righteousness in it. We agree thus far. I think we may go thus far further, that we all apprehend danger from the person of the King, and from the Lords. All that have spoke have agreed in this too. As we do not make it our business or intention to set up the one or the other, so neither is it our intention to preserve the one or the other with a visible danger and destruction to the people and the public interest. So that that part of difference that seems to be among us is whether there can be a preservation [of them with safety to the Kingdom]. First of all, on the one part, there is this apprehension: that we cannot with justice and righteousness at the present destroy, or go about to destroy, or take away, or lay aside both, or all the interest they have in the public affairs of the Kingdom; and those that do so apprehend would strain something in point of security, would rather leave some hazard to preserve them. On the other hand, those who differ from this [apprehend] that there is not any safety or security to the liberty of the Kingdom, and to the public interest, if you do retain these at all.

As was well said by Lieut. Col. Jubbes, for my part I do not know any outward evidence of what proceeds from the spirit of God more clear than this, the appearance of meekness, and gentleness, and mercy, and patience, and forbearance, and love, and a desire to do good to all, and to destroy none that can be saved. On the other hand, I think that he that would decline the doing of justice – where there is no place for mercy – and the exercise of the ways of force – for the safety of the Kingdom where there is no other way to save it – and would decline these out of the apprehensions of danger and difficulties in it, he doth truly lead us from that which is the law of the spirit of life, the law written in our hearts.

Though God [may] have a purpose to destroy them, and though I should find a desire to destroy them, God can do it without necessitating us to do a thing which is scandalous, or sin, or which would bring a dishonour to his name; and therefore let those that are of that mind wait upon God for such a way when the thing may be done without sin, and without scandal too. On the other hand those who do apprehend obligations lying upon them, that they would clearly come to this resolution, that if they found in their judgments and consciences that those engagements lead to anything which really cannot consist with the liberty and safety and public interest of this nation, they would account the general duty paramount to the other. If we do act according to that mind and that spirit, and that law, and do take these two cautions, God will lead us to what shall be his way.

Bishop: What's the reason that we are distracted in Council, and that we cannot as formerly preserve the Kingdom from that dying condition in which it is? I say it is a compliance to preserve that Man of Blood, and those principles of tyranny which God from Heaven by his many successes hath manifestly declared against.

Wildman: Whatever another man hath received from the spirit, that man cannot demonstrate to me but by some other way than merely relating to me that which he conceives to be the mind of God. We cannot find anything in the word of God what is fit to be done in civil matters. I conceive that only is of God that does appear to be like unto God, justice and mercy, to be meek and peaceable. I should desire therefore that we might proceed only in that way. If it please this honourable Council to consider what is justice and what is mercy, and what is good, and I cannot but conclude that that is of God.

I could much concur that it is very questionable whether

there be a way left for mercy upon that person that we now insist upon. Whether it is demonstrable by reason or justice [that it is right] to punish with death those that according to his command do make war, or those that do but hold compliance with them, and then [to say] that there is a way left for mercy for him who was the great actor of this, and who was the great contriver of all? But I confess because it is in civil matters I would rather look to what is safety.

To give the King a legislative power is contrary to his own oath at his coronation, and it is the like to give a power to the King by his negative voice to deny all laws. And for the Lords, seeing the foundation of all justice is the election of the people, it is unjust they should have that power. Therefore I conceive the difference only is this, whether this power should be given to the King and Lords or no?

Ireton: The question is not whether this should be given to King and Lords or no, but the question is, whether that interest that they have in this (if they have any) should be now positively insisted upon to be clearly taken away.

If we do not expressly take it away, we do leave to them a power to assent or dissent, and give them that which [they] had before. The Parliament have declared it and asserted it, that it is their right that the King ought not to deny any [laws they offer to him]; it is his oath. They have gone thus much farther, that if he did not confirm them they were laws without him. Upon this there hath been a war made. Now if the King by his act do confirm what the Parliament have done, and condemn all that have been against the Parliament, whether he do not acknowledge to all posterity, that in case of safety, when the Parliament doth adjudge the safety of the Kingdom to be concerned they are to make a law without him? For my part I think there can be nothing more clear than this is.

[*The proposals drawn up the committee on Sunday were read.*]

Ireton: It gives the negative voice to the people; no laws can be made without their consent. And secondly it takes away the negative voice of the Lords and of the King too, as to what concerns the people. All that follows for the King or Lords is this, that the Lords or King are not bound by that law they pass for their own persons or estates as the Commons are, unless they consent to it. Therefore what is there wanting for the good or safety of the Commons of England?

Tichborne: I do remember on Saturday last we were at this pitch: that all the power of making laws should be in those that the people should choose; the King and Lords should serve only to this end, that laws should be presented to them, that if they would do the Commons that right as to confirm those laws they should do it; but if they should not think fit to sign them, it should beget a review of that by the House of Commons; and if after a review the House of Commons did declare that was for the safety of the people, though neither King nor Lords did subscribe, yet it was a standing and binding law; and therefore we shall not need to fear to take a shadow when they can do us little hurt.

Ireton: [The committee decided instead that the Lords should have not even a suspensive veto where the safety of the Kingdom was concerned, but only a power to nullify certain laws in so far as they affected their own persons or estates.]

Wildman: It will never satisfy the godly people in the Kingdom unless that all Government be in the Commons, and freely. According to what is there propounded the power of the House of Commons is much lessened – from what it is of right, not from what it is now by usurpation of King and Lords. Whereas it's said, that no law shall be made without the consent of the Commons, it doth suppose some other lawmakers besides the representative of the Commons.

Ireton: I do not find that the gentleman that speaks of them doth show what was the ancient constitution, nor of that usurpation, but only [the evidence] of the King's oath. These two powers of the legislative power and the judicial have been exercised between both Lords and Commons, and none of them to exercise the one or the other without mutual consent.

Rainborough: That the Commissary General [*Ireton*] [should be] willing to lay that of constitution aside, and that of custom aside, and to consider the equality and reasonableness of the thing, and not to stand upon constitution, which we have broken again and again.

Ireton: I wish but this, that we may have a regard to safety – safety to our persons, safety to our estates, safety to our liberty. Let's have that as the law paramount, and then let us regard positive constitution as far as it can stand with safety to these.

The Government of Kings or of Lords is as just as any in the world, is the justest Government in the world. Here hath been agreements of the people that have agreed with this. There hath been such an agreement when the people have fought for their liberty, and have established the King again.

Wildman: They were cozened as we are like to be.

Ireton: I would not have you talk of principles of just

government when you hold that all governments that are set up by consent are just. [Argue instead for] such or such a way that can consist with the liberty of the people. That's one maxim, that all government must be for the safety of the people.

If God will destroy King or Lords he can do it without our or your wrongdoing. The King and Lords are suable, impleadable in any court. The King may be sued and tried by a jury, and a Lord may be sued and tried per Pares only, a knight by esquires. What needs more where there are such laws already that the King and Lords are so bound?

Wildman: Whether it be a shadow or no, I think it is a substance when nothing shall be made but by address to the King. This will be very shameful in future chronicles, that after so much blood there should be no better an issue for the Commons.

The end of the Debates

The General Council's meetings of 28 October and 1 November had made clear that further meetings were likely to be unhelpful without preparatory work by the committee. Thereafter, General Council meetings were interspersed with committee meetings in an attempt to agree terms for a political settlement on which the whole Army could agree, but only a few fragments of the debates on these days are recorded. It is not even known whether the new agents and their civilian friends attended after 1 November. The committee's draft of 2 November adopted some proposals from the *Agreement*, including the idea of rights reserved from the Commons, to include matters of religion and the soldiers' indemnity. The General Council met on the same day and endorsed the proposals, but there is uncertainty over what it agreed about the franchise: probably it confirmed the decision made at the informal meeting on 29 October – the franchise for all except servants and beggars.

When the General Council met on 5 and 6 November, with Fairfax presiding, it was still unable to complete the draft terms for a settlement. Negotiations with the King seem to have remained the most divisive issue. On 5 November, during Cromwell's absence at the Commons, Rainborough managed to persuade the General Council to send a letter to the Speaker declaring that the Army did not support any further addresses to the King, upon which Ireton walked out.

After 6 November Fairfax and Cromwell seem to have changed their strategy, abandoning the attempt to draw up detailed settlement terms endorsed by a General Council. They may have despaired of securing agreement, despite the many concessions to the radicals, and may have been aware of the King's intention to escape from Hampton Court, making settlement terms pointless. Perhaps they regarded what had already been agreed (for example on the franchise) as too radical to form the basis of an agreed settlement. But the main reason may well have been growing division in the Army, which the debates in Putney were perhaps exacerbating. For the Army was clearly now threatened both from without and within: not only were the Levellers stirring up mutiny but part of one regiment had declared for the King. The immediate issue was no longer the details of a constitutional settlement but control of the Army.

When the General Council met on 8 November Cromwell began by attacking the principles of those who he said were seeking to divide the Army, and singled out the *Agreement*'s implication of all men having the vote as tending towards anarchy (despite the compromise apparently agreed earlier). This indicated that he was no longer seeking a consensus encompassing the new agents and Levellers. He then moved that, in view of Fairfax's intention to call a general rendezvous of the Army and the 'distempers' in several regiments, the agitators should return to their regiments until summoned again. There was apparently no opposition, probably because all ranks, even if they supported specific radical proposals, shared a fear that discipline was breaking down.

At its last meeting, on 9 November, the General Council appointed another committee, to assist Fairfax in drawing up the summary of the Army's aims which he was to put to the regiments. Extraordinarily it included Wildman. The partial record of the committee's meeting on 11 November (at Mr Chamberlain's) includes the following:

Colonel Harrison: That the King was a Man of Blood, and therefore the engagement taken off, and that they were to prosecute him.

Cromwell: Answered him by putting several cases in which murder was not to be punished. Stated the case of David upon Joab's killing of Abner, that he spared him upon two prudential grounds: one that he would not hazard the spilling of more blood in regard the sons of Zeruiah were too hard for him.

Ireton: Answered in the same case, and further urged this, that we are not to sin, or to go in any unlawful way to do that which is for bringing a delinquent to judgement.

Fairfax: That we do but secure the King in the right of another [*i.e. the Parliament*].

Cowling: It was his usurping power in the law that would have ruined us, and do but destroy that and let his person alone, we care not for it.

On the same day the King escaped from Hampton Court, on 13 November Fairfax left Putney for the first rendezvous, and on 17 November Army headquarters left Putney.

Cromwell later told the Commons that the reason he had treated the Levellers as he had was that he had hoped that 'their follies would vanish, but now when he sees they spread and infected so much he confesses it high tyme to suppress such attempts. And for a more equall representative, because he saw many honest officers were possest with it, he gave waye to dispute about it at the Counsell of War, partly to persuade them out of the unreasonablenes of that representation these London Agents would have', but when he saw that they would include even beggars in the franchise he had opposed them. For Cromwell and others, the possible expansion of the franchise clearly remained a worrying issue.

After the Debates

Mutiny at Ware

The unity of 8 November quickly evaporated. By about 11 November, *A copy of a letter sent by the agents of severall regiments*, subscribed to by Sexby among others, was being distributed in the Army and in London. It charged the officers with apostasy and called on soldiers to disobey the order for three separate rendezvous and to gather in a single one – in effect to mutiny. But the ill-organised mutiny by two regiments at the first rendezvous at Ware was quickly suppressed, and other regiments declared their loyalty and in many cases expressed revulsion against attempts to split the Army. Order and discipline were restored.

The *Remonstrance* which each regiment was asked to subscribe to at the three rendezvous on 15-18 November condemned the new agents and their friends for seeking to divide the Army and reiterated the material and political aims the Army had been pursuing since June. It left other questions, including by implication the franchise and the negative voice of King and Lords, to Parliament to determine.

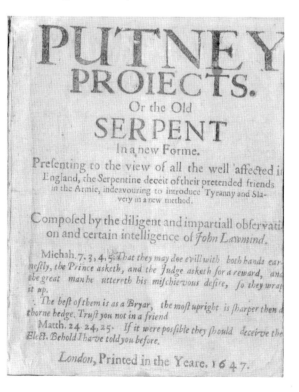

Fig. 23. The title page of Putney Projects, of December 1647, written by Wildman under the pseudonym or anagram John Lawmind. It is a fierce attack on Cromwell and Ireton for their dealings with the King and Parliament, accusing them of seeking to reintroduce tyranny and slavery.

The General Council meeting on 9 November seems to have been the last at which soldier agitators participated, and the unique experiment of July 1647 therefore came to an end. Indeed from the time of the Putney Debates the idea of a General Council was associated, somewhat unfairly, with mutiny. The General Council, including officer agitators but not soldier agitators, continued to meet occasionally until 8 January 1648, but it now concentrated on material matters such as pay and disbandment. Nevertheless, during its short life the General Council had contributed significantly to the Army's cohesion and to the political education which would enable it to take control of events in late 1648. And the political programme adopted by the Army in late 1648 owed much to the ideas debated at Putney.

As for the individual participants in the Putney Debates, no-one appears to have suffered for the views expressed. The most remarkable case is that of Sexby, who was used by the Army's leaders as an intermediary in 1648 and eventually rose to command a regiment. William Allen also became an officer.

Levellers and Army in 1648-9

The Putney Debates attract attention because of the fierce disagreements, but in fact the Army came far closer to adopting and implementing Leveller ideas in late 1648. After the Second Civil War of March-August 1648, when the Army defeated both English and Welsh Royalists and a Scottish army called into England by the King, the Army again confronted a hostile Parliament dominated by Presbyterians. It reacted in December by drastically purging Parliament and preparing to try the King. The most divisive issue at Putney was thus to be resolved in the most radical way possible. The Army was politically much more isolated than it had been in 1647, and was badly in need of friends.

While putting together a draft Remonstrance in November 1648, the Army received proposals from the Levellers and radical Independents, and agreed to a suggestion from the Leveller leader, John Lilburne, for a committee consisting of four from each faction – Levellers, Army, London Independents and the 'honest party' in Parliament. The Remonstrance was amended to include many ideas from the *Agreement*, including a new constitution based on agreement, a 'supreme council or parliament' elected yearly or biennially 'with as much equality as may be', and only those who subscribed to the *Agreement* eligible to engage in politics.

In December the committee proposed by Lilburne drew up a new version of the *Agreement*, in which it dealt with the problem that a free election would undoubtedly lead to a royalist Parliament. All male householders over 21 were to be eligible to vote provided they signed the *Agreement*, had not given aid or comfort to the royalist cause or joined in opposition to the *Agreement* (in which case they were to be excluded for seven years), and were 'not persons receiving Alms, but such as are assessed ordinarily towards the relief of the poor; not servants to, or receiving wages from any particular person'. This was a wide franchise, but less so than the one agreed at Putney, since it was confined to ratepaying householders and excluded many potential electors on political grounds. Ireton, who played a central role in this, had clearly seen that the Leveller ideas of subscription to the constitution and reserved powers were a defence against a return of the monarchy. Reserved powers included liberty of conscience in religion and interference with property rights.

When the Council of Officers examined the committee's document, they removed the requirement for everyone to sign the *Agreement* (it was enough for voters not to oppose it) and removed the reserve on religion, but provided that Parliament should have no power in 'things Spirituall or Evangelicall'. No change was made to the provisions on the franchise. This new version of the *Agreement* was presented to the Commons on 20 January 1649, but that was that: the Commons never did consider it, and the Army never reminded the Commons about it. Its most consistent supporters were the lower officers of the Army, whereas the Army rank and file and the Independent congregations of London seem to have had little interest in it.

The Levellers did not forget it, and their increasingly intemperate attacks on the Army's leadership and attempts to stir up mutiny created an irreconcilable gulf between Army and Levellers in 1649. The Leveller leaders were imprisoned and the mutinies were crushed.

1648-9 was the high point for major constitutional change: the monarchy and the House of Lords were abolished, but the possibility of reforming the Commons and the franchise disappeared (apart from a short-lived redistribution of parliamentary seats in 1654-9) and did not reappear for nearly two centuries. Much of the 1650s was spent re-establishing elements of the traditional political system in an attempt to broaden the regime's base of support, and in 1660 the monarchy was restored. The specific Leveller demands, such as the enlarged franchise, disappeared from view. Indeed by 1688 radical reformers, including Wildman, wanted a *narrower* franchise so that votes could not be bought by the rich. What survived, though bitterly contested, was the idea that ordinary men and women could claim a significant voice in politics and make demands of the Government, together with an increased willingness among them to do so.

The transcript and its rediscovery

The Putney Debates were not public ones, and were scarcely even mentioned in contemporary newspapers. The term 'Putney Debates' was not used until centuries later. Without the transcript we would have almost no idea about what had taken place. While the Debates were forgotten, the shorthand notes made by William Clarke, secretary to the General Council, survived, and so, for a time, did Clarke himself. Clarke served under General Monck in Scotland in the 1650s, and returned with him to London in January 1660, shortly before Monck brought about the Restoration. In 1661 Clarke was knighted and became secretary-at-war. He began making a fair copy of all his shorthand notes, including the Putney ones in

Fig. 24. William Clarke (1623/4-66), secretary to the Army's General Council. (Miniature by Samuel Cooper.)

1662, probably as a deliberate attempt to preserve the record for posterity; the shorthand notes themselves he destroyed. Making the fair copy evidently caused him some difficulty, not only because the systems of shorthand available were not yet very effective but probably also because there had been more than one shorthand writer at Putney, and parts of the transcript are hard to interpret. One can only wonder what Clarke thought of the views expressed in such utterly different political circumstances 15 years earlier.

In 1666 Clarke was killed at sea in the Four Days' Fight during the Second Anglo-Dutch War, aged only 43. In 1736 his son bequeathed his papers and books, including the Putney transcript, to Worcester College, Oxford. There the transcript remained unknown until the college librarian brought it to the attention of a young historian, Charles Firth, in about 1890. Firth published it, with other material, in 1891. The Levellers began to be rediscovered by historians in the 1890s. But it was not until 1938, when A.S.P. Woodhouse published a new, more accessible version of the transcript, rather freely edited, in a volume entitled *Puritanism and liberty*, that the Putney Debates first entered popular consciousness. There for the first time the term 'Putney Debates' was used, and as such they have continued to be well-known ever since.

Conclusion

What makes the Putney Debates so exciting is the freedom from deference to tradition, to rank and to established authority, together with the fact that it was a genuine debate between strongly opposed viewpoints. The franchise may not have been central to the search for a settlement, but nevertheless it *was* debated at length at Putney, and with passion. Other issues debated at Putney, notably the accountability of rulers for their actions and the concept of reserved powers, also continue to be live ones today. It is impressive that, even in such unpromising soil as seventeenth-century England had been, ideas such as the sovereignty of the people could be so confidently proclaimed almost as soon as the restraints were lifted.

Cromwell was of course right that the sort of constitution proposed in the *Agreement*, including the wider franchise, could have been established at the time only by force, against the will of the House of Commons, and that it might well have been rejected by a population desperate for a more settled, less intrusive and less expensive government. The wider franchise might also have had unintended consequences, such as a royalist Parliament or greater opportunity for the rich to buy votes. But it is possible to acknowledge Cromwell's case even while continuing to be moved by Rainborough's plea for 'the poorest he' and by the emphasis on the sovereignty of the people.

Centuries later we enjoy the democratic franchise and, in effect, the sovereignty of the people called for in 1647, but they took a long time to achieve. The argument which started at Putney in 1647 continued for centuries in Britain and remains unfinished even today in many countries. Whereas in the late twentieth century countries with no experience of democracy were able to adopt it and make it work partly because they had examples of successful democracies to follow, in the seventeenth century there were no such examples, and much political education and struggle were necessary before there could be. Those arguing at Putney for a democratic franchise were the first in modern history anywhere in the world to attempt this political education, and that is what makes the Putney Debates so enduringly important.

Appendix 1

An Agreement of the People

An agreement of the people, for a firm and present peace, upon grounds of common right.

Having by our late labours and hazards made it appear to the world at how high a rate we value our just freedom, and God having so far owned our cause as to deliver the enemies thereof into our hands: we do now hold ourselves bound in mutual duty to each other to take the best care we can for the future, to avoid both the danger of returning into a slavish condition and the chargeable remedy of another war; for as it cannot be imagined that so many of our countrymen would have opposed us in this quarrel if they had understood their own good, so may we safely promise to ourselves that when our common rights and liberties shall be cleared, their endeavours will be disappointed that seek to make themselves our masters; since therefore our former oppressions and scarce yet ended troubles have been occasioned either by want of frequent national meetings in council or by rendering those meetings ineffectual, we are fully agreed and resolved to provide that hereafter our representatives be neither left to an uncertainty for the time, nor made useless to the ends for which they are intended; in order whereunto we declare:

I.

That the people of England, being at this day very unequally distributed by counties, cities & boroughs for the election of their deputies in Parliament, ought to be more indifferently proportioned, according to the number of the inhabitants; the circumstances whereof, for number, place and manner, are to be set down before the end of this present Parliament.

II.

That to prevent the many inconveniences apparently arising from the long continuance of the same persons in authority, this present Parliament be dissolved upon the last day of September which shall be in the year of our Lord 1648.

III.

That the people do of course choose themselves a Parliament once in two years, viz. upon the first Thursday in every 2nd March, after the manner as shall be prescribed before the end of this Parliament, to begin to sit upon the first Thursday in April following at Westminster, or such other place as shall be appointed from time to time by the preceding representatives, and to continue till the last day of September then next ensuing and no longer.

IV.

That the power of this and all future representatives of this nation is inferior only to theirs who choose them, and doth extend, without the consent or concurence of any other person or persons, to the enacting, altering and repealing of laws, to the erecting and abolishing of offices and courts, to the appointing, removing and calling to account magistrates and officers of all degree, to the making war and peace, to the treating with foreign states, and generally to whatsoever is not expressly or implyedly reserved by the represented to themselves.

Which are as followeth:

1. That matters of religion, and the ways of God's worship, are not at all intrusted by us to any humane power, because therein we cannot remit or exceed a tittle of what our consciences dictate to be the mind of God without wilful sin; nevertheless the public way of instructing the nation (so it be not compulsive) is referred to their discretion.

2. That the matter of impresting and constraining any of us to serve in the wars is against our freedom, and therefore we do not allow it in our representatives, the rather because money (the sinews of war) being always at their disposal, they can never want numbers of men apt enough to engage in any just cause.

3. That after the dissolution of this present Parliament, no person be at any time questioned for anything said or done in reference to the late public differences, otherwise than in execution of judgments of the present representatives, or House of Commons.

4. That in all laws made, or to be made, every person may be bound alike, and that no tenure, estate, charter, degree, birth or place do confer any exemption from the ordinary course of legal proceedings whereunto others are subjected.

5. That as the laws ought to be equal, so they must be good, and not evidently destructive to the safety and well-being of the people.

These things we declare to be our native rights, and therefore are agreed and resolved to maintain them with our utmost possibilities against all opposition whatsoever, being compelled thereunto not only by the examples of our ancestors, whose blood was often spent in vain for the recovery of their freedoms, suffering themselves, through fraudulent accommodations, to be still deluded of the fruit of their victories, but also by our own woeful experience, who, having long expected

69

& dearly earned the establishment of these certain rules of government, are yet made to depend for the settlement of our peace and freedom upon him that intended our bondage and brought a cruel war upon us.

[The *Agreement* was accompanied by letters from the new agents to the people of England and to Fairfax and fellow-soldiers. The letter to the people included the following:]

But if any shall enquire why we should desire to join in an Agreement with the people, to declare these to be our native rights, & not rather petition to the Parliament for them, the reason is evident: no Act of Parliament is or can be unalterable, and so cannot be sufficient security to save you or us harmless from what another Parliament may determine, if it should be corrupted; and besides, Parliaments are to receive the extent of their power and trust from those that betrust them; and therefore the people are to declare what their power and trust is, which is the intent of this Agreement.

[The signatories of the letter were Edmund Bear and Robert Everard of Cromwell's regiment, George Garret and Thomas Beverley of Ireton's regiment, William Pryor and William Bryan of Fleetwood's regiment, Matthew Weale and William Russell of Whalley's regiment and John Dover and William Hudson of Rich's regiment.]

Appendix 2

Participants in the Debates

These are only the participants who spoke during the three recorded days. It was undoubtedly the most remarkable group of men ever assembled at Putney. Many of them were recently promoted in October 1647 following the upheavals which had caused the departure of many officers from the Army. Sons of gentlemen sat side by side with shoemakers and button-sellers. Their careers after the Debates varied greatly: some sank into obscurity; others continued in military or naval careers or were otherwise engaged in political or religious activity. Seven signed the death warrant of Charles I. Following the Restoration, one (Hugh Peter) was executed, two spent the rest of their lives in prison and two fled abroad. Some remained true to a set of political or religious principles, whereas others radically changed their views, a few even becoming Royalists or Catholics.

Captain Francis Allen. Officer agitator. Still in the Army in 1658, when he became a Lieutenant-Colonel.

William Allen. Soldier agitator. From Warwickshire; a feltmaker in Southwark. Enlisted 1642; wounded at Newbury and Henley. A founder of the Particular Baptist Church at Dalwood, Devon, in 1645-8. Accompanied Cromwell to Ireland 1649 and rose to be adjutant-general. Became a committed republican. Resigned his commission 1656. Given command of a regiment by the Rump Parliament 1660. Imprisoned 1660-1 and required to go into exile. Last heard of 1667.

Captain Lewis Audley. Officer agitator. Probably the son of a Marlborough linendraper. Remained in the Army until at least 1651. An unsuccessful parliamentary candidate in 1658. Helped prevent a gathering of Royalists in Surrey in 1659.

'Bedfordshire man'. One of the new agents, from Whalley's regiment.

Captain George Bishop. Officer agitator. From Bristol. After 1647 embarked on a new career providing domestic intelligence for the Council of State. Became a Quaker 1654. From 1655 issued a series of appeals to Cromwell, the army, Parliament and Charles II, generally prophesying the imminent judgment of the Lord but also emphasising liberty of conscience. Died 1668.

Captain-Lieutenant William Bray. Officer agitator. The only person recorded as challenging Cromwell's assertion at Putney on 8 November 1647 that a universal franchise meant anarchy. During the Leveller-inspired mutiny at Ware in

November 1647 Bray was the only officer above the rank of lieutenant who stayed with the troops. Court-martialled, but pardoned on expressing remorse. Expelled from the Council of Officers and cashiered in March 1649 for defending soldiers' right to petition and attacking Fairfax; imprisoned 1649-51. Remained a Leveller, and wrote a pamphlet on behalf of the 'Good Old Cause' in 1659.

Captain John Carter. Officer agitator. Captain from 1645. As lieutenant-colonel, resigned in 1651 to avoid court-martial for tippling. Probably the same man who commanded a regiment in the West Indies 1654-5. Died 1655.

Lieutenant Edmund Chillenden. Officer agitator. Son of a Faversham yeoman. A button-seller in London 1637. Distributing subversive puritan literature with the future Leveller leader, John Lilburne, 1638. Arrested as a member of a separatist congregation in 1641. In the parliamentary army from 1642. Supported the *Agreement of the People*, but lost sympathy with the Levellers. Published a defence of 'Preaching without Ordination' in 1647. Fought in the Second Civil War and in Scotland. Increasingly devoted himself to theology, and by 1653 was leader of a General Baptist congregation meeting in part of St Paul's Cathedral and known as 'Captain Chillenden's Church'; doctrinally Fifth Monarchist. Cashiered from the Army and expelled from his church (temporarily) in 1653 for getting his maid pregnant. Briefly rejoined the Army 1660. A coffee-house keeper in Leadenhall Street by 1661, and was arrested for publishing illegal newspapers 1677-8, 40 years after he had first done so.

Captain John Clarke. Officer agitator. In Ireland as lieutenant-colonel from 1651, and retained command of a regiment there until 1659. Sat in all the Protectorate Parliaments.

Nicholas Cowling, Commissary-General of Victuals. Officer. Son of a Somerset gentleman. The main proponent at Putney of the Leveller view of the 'Norman yoke' as the origin of oppression. Probably left the Army 1648.

Lieutenant-General Oliver Cromwell. Officer. Born 1599 at Huntingdon, son of a gentleman. An MP in 1628 and from 1642. An army officer from 1642; Lieutenant-General of the horse in the New Model Army from 1645; succeeded Fairfax as the Army's commander 1650. Fought at Marston Moor, Naseby, Langport, Preston, Drogheda, Dunbar and Worcester. Lord Protector from 1653. Refused the Commons' offer of the crown 1657. Died 1658.

Adjutant-General Richard Deane. Officer. Born 1610 in Gloucestershire; related to Cromwell. Possibly a merchant. In the army from 1642. Comptroller of the ordnance in the New Model Army from 1645; adjutant-general 1647. Closely allied to Cromwell. Active in the trial of Charles I and signed the death warrant. One of the three commissioners in charge of the fleet from 1649, but also fought on

Fig. 25. Adjutant-General Richard Deane.

land in Scotland. Killed by the Dutch at the Battle of Solebay 1653. Buried in Westminster Abbey but at the Restoration his bones were thrown into the adjacent churchyard. A puritan, with a strong mystical streak.

Captain Denne. Unidentified. Perhaps the Cornet Henry Den who was a ringleader of the Burford mutiny in 1649 and later a Baptist preacher.

Robert Everard. One of the new agents. A trooper in Cromwell's cavalry regiment by autumn 1647. A signatory to the *Agreement of the People*, and presented it to Army headquarters at Putney 1647. Recorded as 'Buff-Coat' in the Putney Debates transcript. Involved in Leveller mutinies 1649, but probably remained in the Army until 1651. Became a Baptist and published pamphlets. By 1664 had been converted to Catholicism.

Lieutenant-Colonel William Goffe. Officer agitator. Son of a Sussex clergyman. Apprenticed to a London grocer 1634. Fought in Essex's army. A captain in the New Model Army from 1645; lieutanant-colonel 1647. A political and religious radical, with a strong millenarian conviction that he was living through the last days of human history. Already in favour of trying the King 1647, and signed Charles I's death warrant. Strong supporter of Cromwell and later Richard Cromwell. Major-General for Berkshire, Sussex and Hampshire 1655. Cashiered May 1659. Exempted from the Act of Indemnity and Oblivion 1660 as a regicide and fled to Massachusetts, where he lived in hiding, in a cave for about three years and then in the house of a Minister. Said to have defended Hadley, Massachusetts, against Indians 1675. Died c.1679.

Fig. 26. Colonel John Hewson.

Colonel John Hewson. Officer. A shoemaker in Westminster in the 1630s. In the army from 1642; colonel in the New Model Army from 1645. Involved in Pride's Purge 1648 (when the Commons Members likely to oppose the King's trial were excluded), and signed Charles I's death warrant 1649. A religious radical, but an opponent of the Levellers; helped crush them at Burford 1649. In Ireland 1649-56. Became Lord Hewson in Cromwell's new second chamber of Parliament 1658. Deprived of his command December 1659. Fled abroad 1660 and died about 1662.

Commissary-General Henry Ireton. Officer. Born 1611 in Nottinghamshire; son of a gentleman. An officer in the army from 1642. Commissary-General of the Horse in the New Model Army (second in command of the cavalry) from 1645. Married Cromwell's daughter Bridget in 1646; a close ally of Cromwell. Drew up the Army's Heads of Proposals in 1647 as the basis for a settlement with the King. Politically conservative at Putney, but events pushed him towards greater radicalism; a leading figure in the events leading to the King's execution and signed the death warrant. Second in command under Cromwell in Ireland from 1649, and in command from 1650. Died there of fever in 1651.

Lieutenant-Colonel John Jubbes. Officer agitator. Apparently from Norfolk. Entered the army as a captain 1643; lieutenant-colonel in the New Model Army from 1645. Became disillusioned with Cromwell and the other officers and resigned his commission 1648. Promoted a moderate version of the *Agreement of the People*, including the restoration of Charles I. Died in Jamaica 1658.

Lieutenant-Colonel Henry Lilburne. Officer agitator. Younger brother of the Leveller leader, John Lilburne. An officer from 1644; lieutenant-colonel 1647. In August 1648, as Governor of Tynemouth Castle, suddenly declared for the King, and was killed during the Castle's recapture.

Nicholas Lockyer. Soldier agitator. Lieutenant 1653; a commissioned officer 1659. Led a rising in Nottinghamshire in April 1660 in support of General Lambert when Charles II's Restoration was virtually certain.

Captain John Merriman. Officer agitator. Captain 1647. In 1648 was sent to remove the King from the Isle of Wight to Hurst Castle. In Scotland in the mid-1650s. Called out of retirement in June 1659 to be a major (after the fall of Richard Cromwell).

Hugh Peter. Civilian. Born in Cornwall 1598, son of a merchant. Clergyman from 1623, but his licence to preach was suspended 1627. Thereafter generally in the Netherlands and then in New England 1635-41, after which he returned to England. Became a major promoter of Parliament's cause, mainly through his preaching, which was evidently persuasive, but also through his aptitude for practical organisation. In 1647 championed the Independents and the Army. Supported the King's execution. Chaplain to the Council of State from 1650. Published pamphlets advocating a salaried legal profession, publicly-maintained hospitals, homes for orphans, a national bank, canal

Fig. 27. Hugh Peter.

building, abolition of debtors' prisons, freer divorce and university reform. Executed 1660, despite not being a signatory to the King's death warrant.

Maximilian Petty. Civilian. Probably born 1617, son of an Oxfordshire gentleman. Apprenticed to a London grocer 1634. A Leveller, and one of the compilers of the second *Agreement of the People*, 1648. An active member of a republican club 1659-60. Possibly involved in republican plotting in 1661. Possibly the Maximilian Petty of Cliffords Inn, London, who died c.1698.

Colonel Thomas Rainborough. Officer. Son of a merchant and naval officer; grew up in Wapping. A trader in currants with the Turkey Company before 1642. In the navy 1642-3, but from 1643 was a colonel in the army. Fought at Naseby, Langport and Bristol, displaying great courage. An MP from 1647. Increasingly at loggerheads with Cromwell through his opposition to further negotiations with the King and his ambition to become vice-admiral of the navy. When eventually appointed to the navy in January 1648, the navy balked at his radicalism and the men of his own flagship expelled him. Returned to the Army. When about to take over the siege of Pontefract Castle in October 1648, was killed in an attempted kidnap by cavaliers. There was a huge Leveller demonstration at his funeral in London.

Major William Rainborough. Officer agitator. Brother of Thomas. In New England from the late 1630s to 1642. In the navy 1642-3 and in the army as captain from mid-1644; a major from 1647. Dismissed 1649, probably in connection with the Leveller mutiny in the Army. Involved with the Ranters from 1649, and in 1650 was arrested for financing a Ranter pamphlet. Twice nominated for a naval command in the 1650s but vetoed. Appointed colonel of a regiment of militia horse 1659 by the Rump Parliament. Imprisoned 1660-1 on suspicion of treason. Was in Massachusetts 1673.

Lieutenant-Colonel Thomas Reade. Officer agitator. From Wickford, Essex. His father's widow became the first wife of Hugh Peter. A major 1645, and wounded at Taunton. In Scotland from 1650. Re-entered England with Monck in 1660; disbanded with his regiment in October 1660. Died in 1662, as a gentleman of Wickford, Essex.

Colonel Nathaniel Rich. Officer. A gentleman; married John Hampden's sister. In the army from 1642; a colonel in the New Model Army from 1645. Helped draw up the Heads of the Proposals 1647. Reputed a moderate; backed Ireton over the franchise at Putney. Supported religious toleration, and the establishment of a republic. An MP from 1649. Associated with the Fifth Monarchists from 1654. Removed from his command 1654 and became an open opponent of Cromwell; imprisoned 1655-6. Restored to his regiment by the Rump Parliament 1659. Dismissed again 1660 and attempted a last stand against a Restoration. Imprisoned 1661-5. Lived quietly at his ancestral manor of Stondon, Essex. Died c.1701.

Captain Edmund Rolfe. Officer agitator. Born 1619 at Finchley. Apprenticed to a London clothworker 1632. Joined the army 1642; a captain in the New Model Army from 1645. Involved in guarding the King on the Isle of Wight 1648; acquitted following allegations that he had planned to murder the King. Wounds apparently caused his retirement by 1654. Living in London at the time of his death c.1668.

Edward Sexby. Soldier agitator. From Suffolk. Joined Cromwell's Ironsides 1643. In April 1647 interrogated by the Commons over his part in the *Apologie of the Common Soldiers*, the first manifesto of the ordinary soldiers. Played a major part in organising the agitators, and became an intermediary between the General Council and the new agents. Apparently left the Army in late 1647. Used as an intermediary by the Army's leaders 1648. Back in the Army 1649 and rose to Colonel. Cashiered for detaining the pay of some of his soldiers 1651. Was sent to France 1651-3 to promote rebellion there; helped draw up a French version of the

Agreement of the People; fled 1653. Turned against Cromwell and the Protectorate, and following an attempt to arrest him in 1655 he fled to Flanders. There he made contact with Royalists and negotiated with Spain for support for risings in England to restore Charles II. Promoted Sindercombe's plot 1657. Published *Killing noe murder*, arguing for tyrannicide and placing Cromwell on a par with Caligula and Nero. Arrested in England 1657 and died in the Tower 1658.

Colonel Robert Tichborne.

Officer. Born 1610/11 in London; son of a gentleman. A wealthy linendraper in Cheapside 1642. Captain in the London trained bands 1642; lieutenant-colonel of a regiment of London auxiliaries 1643. Became a leader of the City's Independents against the Presbyterians. When the Army occupied London in August 1647 he became a colonel and lieutenant of the Tower. Signed Charles I's death warrant. Held various offices from 1649, and was Lord Mayor of London 1656. In Cromwell's House of Lords 1657. Sentenced to death as a regicide in 1660, but imprisoned instead until 1682, dying in the Tower.

Fig. 28. Colonel Robert Tichborne.

Sir Hardress Waller.

Officer. Born c. 1604 in Kent, a gentleman. Lived on his Irish estates from about 1630, and became a colonel in the army set up to crush the Irish rebellion of 1641; was in Oxford lobbying the King against making peace with the Irish rebels 1644, but fled to London in August 1644. A colonel in the New Model Army from 1645. Became a religious Independent and a supporter of Cromwell. Involved in Pride's Purge 1648 and signed Charles I's death warrant. With the army in Ireland from 1649, and was granted Irish lands in 1657. Staged an unsuccessful anti-Royalist coup in Dublin in early 1660. Sentenced to death for regicide, but was instead imprisoned in Jersey, where he died in 1666.

Major Francis White. Officer agitator. First recorded in May 1647 as a captain; a major from June. Expelled from the General Council in September 1647 for arguing that there was now no visible authority in the Kingdom but the sword; nevertheless felt able to attend the meeting at Putney on 29 October; readmitted

December 1647. Supported the Levellers, prompting the suspension of his commission in September 1648. But opposed the King's execution, arguing that he should only be deposed. Was sent to mediate with the Leveller mutineers in 1649 and unwittingly led them into a trap at Burford. Lieutenant-colonel 1650. An MP 1656. Sent to Flanders 1657 to be governor of Mardyke Fort. Drowned in a shipwreck 1657.

John Wildman. Civilian. Born 1622/3. Professional plotter, against Cromwell, Charles II, James II and William III. A Leveller leader. May have written the *Agreement*. Author of *Putney Projects*, December 1647. Imprisoned by the Commons 1648. From 1653 generally known as 'the major', though what, if any, army service he had is unclear. Became wealthy through property transactions. Arrested for plotting to assassinate Cromwell 1655; released 1656 apparently in return for agreeing to become a double agent spying on Royalists. Active in 1659-60; seized Windsor Castle on behalf of the Rump Parliament 1660. Imprisoned 1661-7. Abroad 1670-5. An MP 1681. Imprisoned 1683 for involvement in the Rye House plot. Ineffective during Monmouth's Rebellion. In exile 1685-8; involved in the Glorious Revolution. Postmaster-General 1689-91; an MP 1689; a London Alderman 1690-3; knighted 1692. Died 1693.

Army ranks

The general officers included the Commander-in-Chief (Fairfax), the Lieutenant-General (Cromwell), who was second in command and commanded the cavalry, the Commissary-General (Ireton), who was second in command of the cavalry, and more than 20 others, concerned with cavalry, infantry, ordnance, administration or intelligence.

Each regiment was headed by a colonel.

In the cavalry, the colonel was supported by a sergeant major. A regiment had six troops, each of 100 men. A troop had four commissioned officers – a captain, a lieutenant, a cornet and a quartermaster; its non-commissioned officers were three corporals.

In the infantry the colonel was supported by a lieutenant-colonel and a sergeant major. A regiment had ten companies, seven of them with 100 men and the others with up to 200. A company had three commissioned officers – a captain, a lieutenant and an ensign; its non-commissioned officers (in the companies with 100 men) were two sergeants, three corporals and a gentleman-at-arms.

Appendix 3

Officers' billets at Putney and Fulham

Putney

General Fairfax at 'Mr. Wimmersolls' (Wymondsold's). William Wymondsold owned two large houses at Putney in 1636, but there is no evidence of him ever occupying either of them. Fairfax's billet was almost certainly the mansion at the top of the High Street, where Wymondsold was living by 1662. A bitter lawsuit between Wymondsold and Edward Bradbourne, the son-in-law of his former business partner, over this house and other property in 1641 had resulted in victory for Bradbourne, but Wymondsold apparently contrived to keep control of the house.

Commissary General Ireton at Mr Campion's. Three generations of Campions, a London family of brewers, occupied a large house in Putney Bridge Road until 1650.

Colonel Fleetwood at Mr Martin's. James Martyn was occupying a mansion known as Copt Hall by the river in the north-east corner of the parish by 1650.

Scoutmaster General at Mr Hubbert's. Hugh Hubbert was occupying a house on the west side of the High Street near the church by 1662, and had probably obtained it as one of the creditors of Sir Thomas Dawes in the 1640s.

Quartermaster General and Commissary General of Musters at 'Maj. Cumberlins' (Chamberlain's). Philip Burlamachi, financier, had occupied this house until at least 1630, and his son-in-law, Thomas Chamberlain, merchant, was there by 1652.

Lieutenant-Colonel Cowell at Mr Duck's. Dunstan Duck owned a large house on the west side of the High Street near Felsham Road in 1636 and was occupying it in 1652.

Adjutant General of Horse 'at Mr. Cox in the Parke'. Probably Putney Park, where there was a large house (formerly a hunting lodge) in what is now Putney Park Lane.

Commissary General of Victuals at Mr White's. Henry White, landowner, baker, and moneylender, built a house on the east side of the High Street in the 1630s, in which he and then his descendants (the Pettiward family) lived until about 1814.

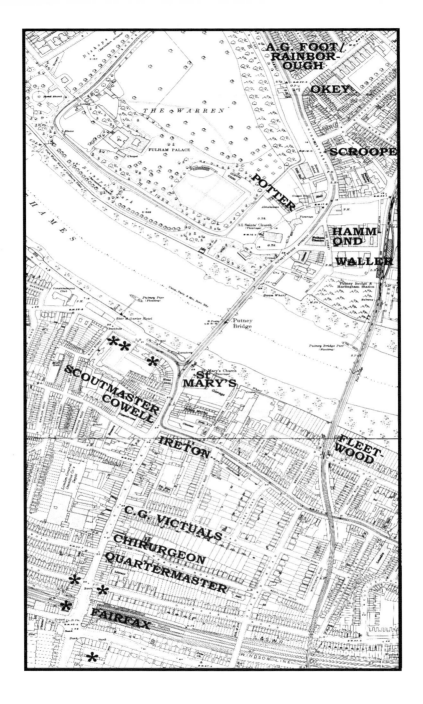

Fig. 30. One of the unwilling hosts of 1647: Henry White of Putney (c.1584-1658), land-owner, baker and moneylender of Putney, seen here in 1654. He accommodated Nicholas Cowling, the Commissary General of Victuals, in 1647.

Fig. 31. The side and back of Fairfax House, Putney High Street, seen from its yard in 1884. The nearer part of the house, with its massive chimneys, was the surviving part of the house built by Henry White in the 1630s. It was demolished in 1887 and Montserrat Road now crosses the site.

Fig. 29 (left). Officers' billets in Putney and Fulham in 1647 and St Mary's church, marked on the Ordnance Survey map of 1913. Other large houses in Putney (except schools) are marked with a star.

81

Chyrurgians and Martial General (Chirurgeon General?) at 'Mr Poller Fenns' (Pollexfen's). Pollexfen was occupying a mansion owned by Wymondsold on the east side of the High Street in 1629, and no other occupant is recorded until 1654.

Mr Bonhunt's, Mr Curley's, Mr Porter's, Mr Allison's and Mr George Smith's cannot be identified.

Fulham

Colonel Sir Hardress Waller at Mr Hill's. Thomas Hill, a writer of court letters (or scrivener), owned and occupied Passor's, now 87 High Street. The property had belonged to Oliver Cromwell's grandfather and then uncle until 1604.

Colonel Hammond at Mr Terrie's. George Terry or Tirrey was Thomas Hill's son-in-law, and was next to Hill in the 1647 rate list. Almost certainly he occupied the house north of Passor's, which was bought by Hill in 1626.

Colonel Twesleday (Twisleton) and Colonel Okey at Mr John Wolverston's. Wolverston, later an Alderman, occupied Cleybroke House on the south side of Fulham Road at its junction with the High Street.

Adjutant General of Foot at Mr Snow's. Edmund Snow leased Holcroft's, on the north side of Fulham Road at its junction with the High Street, in 1646.

Colonel Rainborough at Major Rainborough's. Major William Rainborough is not in the March 1647 rate list, but in May 1649 was in the house which had been Snow's. Possibly Snow had sub-let part of the house in 1647.

Colonel Scroope and Colonel Tomlins at Mr Herbert's. By its placing in the rate lists, the house of Mr James Herbert, merchant, was somewhere on the east side of the High Street a little north from New Kings Road.

Colonel Potter at Mr Sear's. Possibly the house known as Goodriche's, on the north side of Church Row, occupied up to 1643 by Captain John Saris, who was succeeded by his nephew George Sayers or Sairs. Part of the site is now occupied by Sir William Powell's Almshouses.

Further reading

On the New Model Army:

C.H. Firth, *Cromwell's army* (first published 1902).

Ian Gentles, *The New Model Army in England, Ireland and Scotland, 1645-1653* (1992).

M.A. Kishlansky, 'The Army and the Levellers: the roads to Putney', *Historical Journal*, vol. 22 (1979), pp. 795-824.

Keith Roberts, *Cromwell's war machine: the New Model Army 1645-1660* (2005).

On the Putney Debates:

C.H. Firth (ed.), *The Clarke papers: selections from the papers of William Clarke* (2nd edn. 1992). Contains the most reliable transcript of the Putney Debates.

A.S.P. Woodhouse (ed.), *Puritanism and liberty – being the Army Debates (1647-9) from the Clarke manuscripts* (first published 1938). A freer rendering of the transcript than Firth's.

Austin Woolrych, *Soldiers and statesmen: the General Council of the Army and its debates, 1647-1648* (1987). The most detailed account.

Michael Mendle (ed.), *The Putney Debates of 1647: the Army, the Levellers and the English State* (2001). Contains many important essays.

Mark Kishlansky, 'Consensus politics and the structure of debate at Putney', *Journal of British Studies,* vol. 20 (1980-1), pp. 50-69.

Other:

G.E. Aylmer (ed.), *The Levellers in the English Revolution* (1975). Includes the full text of the debate on the franchise at Putney.

Christopher Hill, *God's Englishman: Oliver Cromwell and the English Revolution* (first published 1970).

Christopher Hill, *The world turned upside down: radical ideas during the English Revolution* (first published 1972).

John Morrill (ed.), *Oliver Cromwell and the English Revolution* (1990).

John Morrill, *Oliver Cromwell* (2007). An up-to-date summary (from the *Oxford dictionary of national biography*) in 122 pages.

Keith Thomas, 'The Levellers and the franchise', in G.E. Aylmer (ed.), *The Interregnum: the quest for settlement 1646-1660* (1972).

Sources

Background and **'New agents'** and **Levellers:**
Gentles, *New Model Army*; Woolrych, *Soldiers and statesmen*; Mendle, *Putney Debates*; Kishlansky, 'The Army and the Levellers'.

Putney in 1647:
Dorian Gerhold, *Putney in 1636: Nicholas Lane's map* (1994); Dorian Gerhold, *Putney and Roehampton past* (1994); Dorian Gerhold, *Putney and Roehampton in 1665: a street directory and guide* (2007).

The Debates and **After the Debates:**
Woolrych, *Soldiers and statesmen*; Mendle, *Putney Debates*; Kishlansky, 'Consensus politics'.

Appendix 2:
Richard L. Greaves and Robert Zaller, *Biographical dictionary of British radicals in the seventeenth century* (3 vols., 1982-4); *Oxford dictionary of national biography*; Sir Charles Firth and Godfrey Davies, *The regimental history of Cromwell's army* (2 vols., 1940); Woolrych, *Soldiers and statesmen*.

Appendix 3:
Nicholas Lane's map of Putney; National Archives, Chancery records and hearth tax lists; Northamptonshire Record Office, Wimbledon manor court rolls; Gerhold, *Putney in 1636*; Hammersmith and Fulham Archives, Fulham rate lists and Fèret's extracts from the Fulham court rolls; Charles James Fèret, *Fulham old and new* (3 vols., 1900).

Index